CARING FOR YOUR AGING CAT

A Quality-of-Life Guide for Your Cat's Senior Years

JANICE BORZENDOWSKI

Sterling Publishing Co., Inc.
New York

Photo Credits

Courtesy of Joyce K. Anastasi, pp. 11, 95, 110

Courtesy of MEOW Foundation, pp. 20, 45, 65, 87, 122, 172, 192

Reprinted as a courtesy of, and with permission of, Doctors Foster & Smith, pp. 29, 37

Courtesy of Maureen and John Drexel, p. 56

Courtesy of Debra Severson. p. 69, 176, 178, 202

Courtesy of Micheline Frederick, pp. 136, 138, 163, 186

Courtesy of Susan Bierzychudek, pp. 142, 159

Library of Congress Cataloging-in-Publication Data

Borzendowski, Janice.

Caring for your aging cat : a quality-of-life guide for your cat's senior years / Janice Borzendowski.

p. cm.

Includes index.

ISBN-13: 978-1-4027-2613-2

ISBN-10: 1-4027-2613-9

1. Cats. 2. Cats—Aging. 3. Cats—Health. 4. Veterinary geriatrics. I. Title.

SF447.B637 2006

636.8'08930438—dc22 2006025254

10 9 8 7 6 5 4 3 2 1

Published by Sterling Publishing Co., Inc.
387 Park Avenue South, New York, NY 10016

Distributed in Canada by Sterling Publishing
c/o Canadian Manda Group, 165 Dufferin Street
Toronto, Ontario, Canada M6K 3H6

Distributed in the United Kingdom by GMC Distribution Services

Castle Place, 166 High Street, Lewes, East Sussex, England BN7 1XU
Distributed in Australia by Capricorn Link (Australia) Pty. Ltd.
P.O. Box 704, Windsor, NSW 2756, Australia

Printed in China

Sterling ISBN-13: 978-1-4027-2613-2
ISBN-10: 1-4027-2613-9

For information about custom editions, special sales, premium and corporate purchases, please contact Sterling Special Sales Department at 800-805-5489 or specialsales@sterlingpub.com.

To Auntie Helen: for everything.

To Greta and Beanster: Thanks for keeping me company for so long.

Contents

Acknowledgments

I first must thank Dr. Richard T. Goldston, DVM, ACVIM, of the Parkview Animal Hospital, St. Petersburg, Florida. Called the "father of veterinary geriatrics," Dr. Goldston gave unstintingly of his expertise and materials, and his guidance and information were instrumental to the development of this book.

Thanks, also, to the other veterinarians who took time out of their busy schedules to either meet with me in person or talk with me over the phone: Dr. Josie Beug, DVM, of Five Element Animal Wellness, Miami, Florida; Dr. Grace Bransford, DVM, of the Ross Valley Veterinary Hospital, San Anselmo, California; Dr. Barbara A. Kalvig, DVM, of the New York Veterinary Hospital, New York City; Dr. Diane Levitan, DVM, of the Center for Specialized Veterinary Care, Westbury, New York; and Dr. Molly Rice, DVM, of San Francisco Veterinary Specialists, San Francisco, California. I am very grateful, as well, to the cat lovers whose personal stories of love and care have added so much to this book.

Next I must thank Micheline Frederick and Kerstin Nasdeo, my first readers, and two of the best editors—and the best people—I know. And Julie Trelstad, my editor and my friend: expert at both.

Finally, thanks to my mom, who early on instilled in me and my siblings a love of animals. I am grateful every day for that gift.

Introduction

The first time I saw her, she was displayed as a treasure, nestled in a pair of cupped hands. The hands had opened, like the shell of an oyster, to reveal a solid-gray, palm-sized pearl of a kitten, just six weeks old, with eyes the same color as her fur. Fortunately, the person attached to the hands was not asking a gem-sized price for what she held; in fact, she was giving it away, to the first interested party.

The kitten spent the rest of that day on my desk walking back and forth across the top and "talking," like a professor pacing in front of a blackboard. What, I wondered, could this youngster possibly have to say? At the end of the day, when it came time to box her up for the ride home on the New York City subway, she escalated the volume on her monologue and maintained it all the way home. She was such a captivating speaker, however, that ordinarily self-involved rush-hour riders emerged from behind their paperbacks and newspapers with attentive smiles on their faces. I was even offered a seat—which was just the first of many favors I would be granted by being along for the ride with this outspoken feline.

I named her Greta Graycat, after the Hollywood legend Greta Garbo, for I learned early on that she did not suffer fools gladly, and often preferred to be left alone. And she was not shy about dismissing those she had no time for—in her young years, with a well-aimed, claws-exposed swat. I also realized quickly that she favored men over women and showed better judgment in this regard than I and many of my girlfriends did.

Greta was not the only cat in my life at the time. My childhood cat, Buns, eleven then, was still running my household. She, a singular Siamese, initially did not make Greta feel welcome. But from the beginning Greta had the self-confidence we all long for, and calmly waited out the prerequisite acceptance period. When Buns died two years later, at what I then thought was an old age for cats, Greta took on her role as number-one feline with aplomb. Never would I have imagined she would hold it for nine years longer than her predecessor.

Greta: When you've got it, flaunt it!

When several months later, and without her express permission, I brought home a six-month-old calico from the ASPCA, Greta was even less welcoming than Buns had been to her. She intimidated the newcomer into a corner of the bedroom closet, where Beanster stayed for three weeks, even taking her meals there. Who could blame her? Every time she dared to venture forth, she took one on the chin.

Eventually, though, Greta, sure she had made her point, released Beanster; but Greta's acceptance of her would always remain conditional. Nevertheless, Beanster would never stop trying to earn Greta's approval, and never ceased to forgive Greta's frequent rude rebukes. They eventually became the perfect duo, a sort of bad-cat good-cat combo: one outspoken and often cranky and bossy, the other easygoing—a comedienne, really—who, though totally mute, found other more creative ways to express herself.

From both my "girls" I would learn many practical things: how to find the best seat in the house and never relinquish it; how best to catch and dispatch bugs; that if you keep your hair and nails scrupulously clean, you will be welcome anywhere; that clean laundry hot from the dryer makes the best bed in town; and that you don't have to eat what's put in front of you.

More important were the life lessons I would learn from them: you can make the leap to wherever you want to go in life, if you keep your eye on the prize; when kept waiting, don't get mad, take a nap; keep moving out of the shade and into the sunlight. Most important, they taught me that aging is a gift; and the correct response is, "Thank you, I accept."

Finally, and most pertinent to this book, I learned a lot about how to care for aging cats, for Greta lived to be twenty-two, and Beanster nearly that, living well into her twenty-first year. Like many elderly cats, in her eighteenth year, Greta began to suffer from renal failure. Her vet told me I could keep her alive, probably for another year, by administering subcutaneous fluids every day. The sight of that large needle and "IV" bag unnerved me at first, but no more than the thought of losing Greta. So, after some shaky early efforts—with Greta publicizing her disgust at my clumsiness—"treatment time" provided some of our best moments together. No matter how busy or stressed I was, when I sat with Greta in my lap, the needle in her upper back and the life-extending fluid slowly dripping in, the world went away: it was just me and my cat, she purring and I breathing in time with that most soothing of animal sounds.

Not surprising to me, the vet was wrong about Greta's prognosis, for three years later I was still administering the treatments. But by this time, Greta had grown bone-thin and could hardly see, so even though her vet said I might have another year by adding a second daily treatment and some other medications, I decided to let Greta go—to have her euthanized. I chose as the date the same one on which Buns had died in her sleep, August 8. And I decided to have the procedure carried out in the vet's office, for I wanted my apartment to remain the home where Greta had lived, not died.

Though I had stood as surrogate at the euthanasia of other cats and dogs, for friends who could not bear to do so, when it came Greta's turn I found myself surprised at how peaceful it was—and how fast. I don't know how long I stayed there—long after that still-sleek bundle of fur had grown cold—but it wasn't until I walked away that my heart finally broke, the pieces falling into my shoes, or so it felt, as heavy-footed, I headed home alone.

A year and a month later, Beanster began suffering seizures in the middle of the night, and the next morning I had to have her euthanized; her heart was badly damaged. It was September 11, 2001, and as she died I heard on the radio that the second tower of the World Trade Center was falling. In more ways than one, my world crashed that day. It was difficult to find things to be grateful for in those first hours, but for me, the larger tragedy forced me to focus my attention on arranging food and shelter for those of my friends who worked in the city and could not get home that night to the outer boroughs or the tri-state area. My personal grief would have to wait.

Beanster: Reading between the lines

Grief, as it often does, came in fits and starts, sometimes when I least expected it. I was not surprised to find myself weeping in my first year without the girls every time I opened the door to my apartment after a long day out, still expecting them to be right there, chastising me for being late with their dinner. I was surprised, however, when in conducting the research for this book I found myself reluctant to contact their veterinarian for an interview, afraid to stir up the sadness, four-plus years later. When I finally did, and went to the doctor's office for the first time since Beanster had died, I was relieved she was delayed with a patient, for just stepping through the doorway brought tears to my eyes. And when, coincidentally, I was asked to wait in the very room in which both my girls had died, it was all I could do not to run out.

But I knew it was not just my good fortune that my girls had lived so long; it had, if not everything, a great deal to do with the care that was available and that I was able to give them. Today, high-quality care for aging cats is widely available, and that's the purpose of this book: to share that information with everyone who has the honor and privilege to live with and be loved by a cat, today and for many tomorrows.

HONORING THE COMMITMENT

Caring for an aging cat is not all that different from caring for our own bodies as we go through the various stages of life. A lot of it is common sense, coupled with awareness. When it comes to our own health care, we all know we should go to the dentist regularly to have a checkup and get our teeth cleaned; likewise, we're aware we should have a yearly physical exam, which serves as a baseline to numerous health indicators. We also know the dangers of obesity, and the importance of proper nutrition and exercise to maintaining a healthy weight; and we've been told to watch for the warning signs of various types of cancer, hypertension, diabetes, and countless other diseases and conditions. Some of us are better than others at following through on the medical advice and information we receive; and whether we do or don't is our choice. But our cats have no choice: they're entirely dependent on us for ensuring they receive the proper care and the best chance of a long, healthy life.

Today, plenty of help is available for our aging cats. Advances in veterinary medicine have nearly matched in speed and number those in human medicine. You simply have to learn what's available and how to go about implementing what you learn. This book is set up to guide you through an effective approach to caring for your aging cat.

Part 1, "Understanding the Life of an Older Cat," is designed to introduce you to the basics of caring for your senior feline, beginning with figuring out how old she actually is (you might be surprised), followed by a prevention primer—all-important to ensuring quality of life for as long as your cat lives.

- In Chapter 1, "A Year in the Life of a Cat," you'll learn how to calculate your cat's actual age—not in human terms, but in "cat years"—and how those years translate into changes in your cat's health. You'll also learn about other factors contributing to how a cat ages, in particular, environment and nutrition.
- In Chapter 2, "Prevention: Taking a Proactive Approach to Caring for Your Cat," I'll explain how you can forestall the onset of disease and old-age conditions, or lessen their impact, by following four simple guidelines: pay attention, schedule biannual checkups, plan ahead, and trust your instincts. You'll be introduced to the senior wellness program, and its importance to your cat's health, today and tomorrow.
- In Chapter 3, "Vital Signs: Recognizing Signals of Change from Your Cat," we'll look at both physical and mental signs of your cat's aging body, from cloudy eyes and achy joints to bad breath and weird behavior, and everything in between.

Part 2, "Geriatric Feline Health Care," gets down to the more complicated business of understanding the diseases and ailments a typical aging cat—and you, her owner—may face. The better informed you are about the diseases and disorders associated with the aging cat, the better able you'll be to help provide the care she needs. You are an integral member of your cat's health care team, and her first line of defense.

- In Chapter 4, "Wellness Programs: Keeping Your Cat Healthy for the Long Term," you'll find out why the geriatric-veterinary community prefers to use the term "wellness" when referring to a lifetime of health care for your cat. We'll go into some detail as to the makeup of a standard wellness exam and program, so that you understand fully why it is necessary and how it helps both you and your vet provide your cat with optimum care. But first we'll discuss how to find a veterinarian or evaluate your current vet.
- In Chapter 5, " Keeping Your Cat in Shape: Nutrition, Exercise, and Grooming," you'll find out why it's so important to feed your cat properly; make sure she gets enough exercise, both mental and physical; and take up the slack in her grooming regimen (older cats, especially, have a tendency to let personal hygiene fall by the wayside).
- Chapter 6, "When Your Cat Gets Sick: Understanding Common Age-Related Ailments and Their Treatments," is a primer intended to familiarize you with many of the most common diseases of older cats. You'll read about treatment options, too, including alternative choices.
- Chapter 7, "Dollar Signs: Managing the Costs of Senior Pet Care," addresses the dreaded question: How much is this going to cost me? We'll talk about health insurance for pets, cost-saving programs, and other options for addressing the bottom line.

Part 3, "Quality-of-Life and End-of-Life Issues," helps you face what you may have trouble acknowledging: that you and your cat are coming to the end of your days together.

- In Chapter 8, "Quality of Life: Answering the Hard Questions," we'll address such questions as: How can I tell when my cat is in pain or discomfort? What constitutes quality of life for a cat? We'll talk, too, about *your* quality of life as it relates to caring for your cat, so that you can safely ride the emotional rollercoaster of worry, fear, guilt, and so on.

- Chapter 9, "Farewell, Friend: Coming to Terms with End of Life," helps you face the inevitable: the death of your cat. We'll talk about hospice care for your cat, as important a concept in geriatric pet care as it is in human health care, as well as how to prepare yourself and your family. We'll discuss the difficult topics of euthanasia and "aftercare" (burial versus cremation). Finally, you'll learn how and where to find support for yourself (and your family) during the first difficult days and weeks of coping with the loss of your best friend. Some pet owners are surprised at how deeply affected they are, and for how long, by the death of their cat.
- In the Epilogue, we'll broach the subject of moving forward after the death of your cat, and how that might happen for you.

Throughout the book, you'll also find personal stories from pet owners who have "been there, done that," or are doing it right now—caring for a beloved older cat. You'll be inspired by their efforts and their devotion, and learn from their experiences. Also interspersed throughout the text are sidebars of special or related interest to the subject at hand; "Who's Who" entries identifying pet care groups, organizations, and other resources; and other notes, tips, and items of interest. Each chapter ends with "Key Pet Points," to summarize the important take away concepts from each chapter.

The key point I would like you to take away from this introduction is to begin the process of caring for your older cat by leaving your heart open to the possibility that pet care will come to mean much more than the trips to the vet, a struggle to give medications, the cost to your budget and your peace of mind, and the inevitable disruption to your normal routine. The opportunity to care in this way is a gift, one I believe you will come to cherish.

PART 1

Understanding the Life of an Older Cat

CHAPTER 1

A Year in the Life of a Cat

Joey is a Brooklyn boy, born and raised, but were it not for a lucky choice made by his mother, Joey would have learned early that it's not easy to find decent and affordable housing in the New York City area. Fortunately, Joey's mom was streetwise, as only a Brooklyn girl can be, and had chosen as her maternity ward the underside of a small bush in the backyard of another Brooklyn native—who just happened to be a medical professional with a soft heart. One rainy day in mid-August, shortly after giving birth, the cat seemed determined to make the announcement to her "landlady," who was just arriving home from a shopping trip. As she recounted later, "Mommy Cat greeted me and literally guided me to the side of my house. Underneath a small bush, I saw something tiny, and hardly moving—three small shiny balls of fur. I felt [Mommy Cat] wanted me to be the first to know about her new family."

But after about a week, though Mommy Cat continued to come by every morning for breakfast (she could not be coaxed inside), the kittens had disappeared. It was not until the first week in October, a Sunday, that from her upstairs window, Joey's future caretaker saw Mommy Cat in the yard, and underneath her a little round black-and-white ball—nearly invisible against his mother's similar markings. "I rushed outside, and after feeding them, I wanted to pick up the little guy. I looked at Mommy Cat, and she gave me her approval." (The other two kittens were never seen again.)

From that day forward, Joey began to experience the joys of life in a home of one's own. (His birth mother, who still prefers keeping a distance, has her own "cottage" in the backyard; and, now spayed, no longer has to worry about finding suitable housing for herself and her offspring.) As for Joey, he pays his rent in love and companionship, fair exchange for the run of the house, comfortable places to snooze, plenty of food to eat, attentive medical care, and more toys than most children. And one more thing: He also has a wardrobe. Yes, it turns out Joey is something of a dandy, not uncommon among fashion-conscious New Yorkers. And each year on August 18, Joey gets all dolled up to celebrate his birthday, complete with cone-shaped hat, and enjoys party favors of the feline variety.

Joey, the birthday boy

Joey is one of many felines whose birthday is acknowledged as if he were a human member of the family. According to the American Pet Products Manufacturers Association's (APPMA) 2005–2006 National Pet Owners Survey, approximately 5 percent of the estimated 90 million owned cats in this country have owners who host birthday parties for them. That's a lot of people buying presents (average price $17, reports the APPMA) and/or preparing a special meal to commemorate their cat's birthday. Some greeting-card companies, too, have picked up on the trend and have added pet birthday-card lines.

Thus, it's safe to say that most pet owners know how old their cats are. But do they know how those years translate into changes in a cat's health? Counting the years is not the same as recognizing the effects of those years on a cat's body, and understanding those effects is the first step in learning to care for your aging cat.

When it comes to our own aging process, we humans are acutely aware of every change, real or imagined. Our culture is so age conscious we're bombarded constantly with innumerable products and services that promise to slow, or at least hide, the aging process. We prowl the increasingly long and complex aisles in the drugstore, looking for cosmetics of mass denial; we note every ache and pain, wrinkle and gray hair; and we waste no time in seeking advice and remedies from doctors who specialize in safeguarding even the most remote regions of our bodies from the hands of time.

Who's Who in Pet Health Care: American Pet Products Manufacturers Association (APPMA)

A not-for-profit association for pet product manufacturers and importers, the APPMA conducts industry-related market and scientific research, sponsors educational seminars, and promotes responsible pet ownership. Founded in 1958, today the APPMA's membership is comprised of some 850 companies, from small businesses to major national pet product companies. The association's Web site, www.appma.org, has a lot to offer the general pet-owning public as well.

We're much less attuned to our cat's aging process, however. According to Dr. Richard Goldston, DVM, ACVIM, known as the father of veterinary geriatrics, "the most common mistake people make in evaluating the health of their pets is to assume the problems or signs they see as abnormal in their pets are due to 'just getting old.' When this mistake is made, the pet is frequently not presented to the family veterinarian for a more thorough evaluation."

Vets from around the country concur. Dr. Josie Beug, DVM, a veterinary acupuncturist in Miami, Florida, says, "The biggest

BOODIE'S STORY: SCREAMING FOR ATTENTION

Boodie, a shelter cat, was named Clea upon adoption. But she was rarely if ever called that. Instead, she became Boodie. Why? Who knows why we begin calling our cats by affectionate, often comical, nicknames. It just happens. Usually, a cat that has lived a long life will have acquired several such names, some that last a lifetime, others that parallel a period of the cat's life, as a mark of some funny habit or peculiar behavior, which then falls out of use as the cat ages and the behavior changes.

But Boodie stayed Boodie throughout her long life—though she ever really "boodied up" to only one person: her adoptive mother. A few others she tolerated, but always at a distance. A mostly gray, domestic shorthair, with very subtle hints of calico, Boodie had amber eyes that glowed warmly or were spooky depending on whom she was looking at and whether it was day or night.

Raised in a Queens, New York, apartment, Boodie rarely came in contact with other cats, except for occasional exchanges with the next-door neighbor's cat. So, like many owners of indoor cats, Boodie's owner rarely took her to the vet after she was spayed. There appeared to be no need, and Boodie seemed none the worse for it. In fact, she thrived, even adapting—not without complaint exactly, but with ease—to several moves that might have caused behavior problems in another cat. From Queens to several homes in Connecticut, a bedroom community along the Hudson River, and finally to Atlanta, Georgia, Boodie went along for the ride, as long as her owner was at the wheel. Through job changes and relationship breakups, Boodie was the one constant in her owner's life. She never seemed to change.

Until the day that she did.

Boodie had always had a sharp tongue, especially when she was hungry. Nagging—that was her typical tone. But one day, Boodie—then in her eighteenth year—began to jump on the bed in the morning, stand on her owner's chest, and scream brashly in her face, in an ugly voice new to her repertory. Assuming Boodie was just getting more demanding in her old age, and wanted breakfast *now*, her owner was dismayed when, after getting up to feed her, Boodie ate little more than a bite. And within days, Boodie was refusing to eat at all and began hiding in remote corners of the house.

Having just moved to Atlanta, Boodie's owner was in the difficult position of being in a new city without a veterinarian, so she picked a name out of the Yellow Pages. The vet seemed to focus only on the cat's now-shabby coat, assumed she was dehydrated, and injected her with fluids. No thorough exam was given, no tests were run—the vet didn't even look in Boodie's mouth. Still, Boodie improved slightly—but only for a day. Now scared, Boodie's owner called a second vet. This one wasted no time in finding the problem, for he also wasted no time in opening the cat's mouth: "He literally leaped back in shock when he saw the cancer in her mouth," recalls Boodie's owner. "He said he'd never seen anything as bad, except in textbooks, and that the only kind thing we could do was to end her pain."

Thus, Boodie's owner had no time to prepare to say good-bye to her longtime friend. She said the "vet's physical response at the sight of Boodie's disease" convinced her to have Boodie euthanized immediately.

Afterward, Boodie's owner took her home and buried her in the herb garden, fittingly under a large catnip plant. During the hours of tears she shed that night, and for time to come, Boodie's owner believed she had probably failed to see lots of smaller signs of disease in advance of the dramatic ones.

It was a mistake she would not make again.

mistake is denial, and waiting too long." She adds that "anthropomorphizing," or attributing human characteristics to an animal's behavior, is another common mistake. Dr. Molly Rice, DVM, on the staff at San Francisco Veterinary Specialists, echoes Dr. Beug, saying simply: "Waiting too long to seek treatment is the biggest mistake."

Delaying treatment is, understandably, all too easy to do because, of course, cats don't complain in "human speak," so you might not give more than passing notice for some time to the fact that your cat's tone of voice has changed, along with her eating habits. Sadly, that could also mean she isn't getting the care she needs to ensure she has a long and healthy life.

How can you avoid making this mistake? We'll talk more about this in Chapter 3, "Vital Signs: Recognizing Signals of Change from Your Cat." First, though, you need to figure out how old your cat really is.

Understanding Old Is New

In the past, veterinary health care programs were divided into two categories: young and adult (as opposed to "old") animals. The former involved shots for the pediatric group, followed by booster vaccines for rabies, heartworm, flea control, and so on for adult cats. Recognition came gradually about the different care requirements for older pets—interestingly, as an outgrowth of early studies of human geriatrics—as a distinct field of medical care.

Early on, statements about early human geriatric work were applied directly to dogs (not cats). But, says Dr. Richard Goldston, as specialization in veterinary medicine grew, research in specific organ functions—such as kidney, liver, and heart—"suggested" that older pets might need different levels of medications, since they might not be able to metabolize, or excrete, the normal doses of drugs as effectively as younger animals can.

In 1984, Dr. Goldston established a geriatric wellness program in his private practice and began giving lectures and writing articles on geriatric disorders of dogs and cats. Recognizing his growing expertise, a professional publisher asked him to compile the first comprehensive textbook specifically on the geriatrics of the dog and cat. The result, in 1995, was the publication of *Geriatrics and Gerontology of the Dog and Cat*, co-edited with Johnny Hoskins, DVM, PhD, of Louisiana State University College of Veterinary Medicine.

As a consequence of this groundbreaking publication, veterinary medicine began viewing geriatrics as a distinct "wellness" area, leading to the development of geriatric-specific foods, medicines, diets, and comprehensive health care programs. Soon, geriatrics became, as Dr. Goldston puts it, "the next wave in veterinary medicine across the country and in institutional and industry studies." But as recently as 1999, small animal geriatrics was still considered an emerging market. A walk down the aisles of any pet superstore today would seem to leave no question that it has fully arrived.

Geriatric dogs and cats today comprise the largest caseload percentage in most veterinary practices and hospitals across the country, and veterinary schools routinely offer training in geriatrics.

Who's Who in Pet Health Care: The American Animal Hospital Association (AAHA)

The more than thirty-two thousand members of the American Animal Hospital Association work primarily in the health care of companion animals. These professionals include everyone you'll find in a veterinary clinic, hospital, or office: veterinarians, technicians, managers, receptionists, and others. The AAHA's motto is "Healthy Practices, Healthier Pets." The AAHA Web site is primarily designed for veterinary professionals, but a layperson can learn a lot from a visit there. Go to www.aahanet.org.

CALCULATING THE AGE OF YOUR CAT

Most of us learned that the way to determine a cat's age was to multiply his actual age by seven. That's one of those bits of misinformation that has, over time, acquired the ring of truth—in no small part because it's so easy to remember and has been repeated so many times. But it's not really an accurate way to "date your cat"—though it does serve to make the point that cats age a lot more quickly than we do. And seven is an important number in a cat's life, because it's the age at which most vets consider cats to be at the beginning of old age. But keep in mind a cat's aging process varies by nutrition, environment, and other factors. That is why, when it comes to aging and geriatric pets, the American Animal Hospital Association (AAHA) prefers to use what it calls an *end-of-lifespan percentage*. The association's 2005 "Senior Care Guidelines for Dogs and Cats" recommends that its practitioners apply the guidelines to those animals that are in the last 25 percent of their predicted lifespan for the species and breed.

To determine when you need to start seeking senior care for your cat, you first have to figure out whether he's considered a "senior" (old) or a "geriatric" (very old). The table, at right, "How Old Is Your Cat?" makes it easy for you to do that.

In addition, it's important to recognize three primary factors that impact aging in your cat:

- Genetics
- Environment
- Nutrition

How Old Is Your Cat?

Cat's Age	Human-Equivalent Years
1	15
2	24
3	28
4	32
5	36
6	40
7	44
8	48
9	52
10	56
11	60
12	64
13	68
14	72
15	76
16	80
17	84
18	88
19	92
20	96

Key: Senior Geriatric

Source: Based on a chart developed by Fred L. Metzger, DVM; adapted by William Fortney, DVM, R. T. Goldston, DVM, and Ernest Ward Jr., DVM. Reprinted with permission of Dr. Goldston.

The Gene Factor

People have a tendency to lump dogs and cats together in their minds when it comes to caring for them, simply because they're both domesticated animals that have been sharing our lives with us for so long, often in the same household. (Despite a persistent myth that dogs and cats don't get along, many pet owners have both, though cats outnumber dogs by 20 percent, according to the APPMA.) In fact, unlike dogs, the various members of the cat family are remarkably similar in physiology and behavior. According to Dr. Goldston, dogs and people are more closely linked physiologically than dogs and cats.

Even more important when it comes to care is that cats, says Dr. Goldston, "do not as readily demonstrate their aging process. Cats in general seem to hide their maladies and frequently can become quite sick before their owner notices" (see Boodie's Story, page 13). Furthermore, says Goldston, "Dogs are usually much more active, and more interactive with their human owners, consequently the owner notices much sooner that the dog is acting abnormal, whereas the cat seems to look normal, but just lays around more, assuming an undistressed posture. I believe this is an evolutionary way of cats, as loner animals, not demonstrating their potential weakness to their foes; whereas dogs, as pack animals, are protected by the pack as long as they can just keep up with it." That said, pet cats generally live longer than pet dogs.

When it comes to cat breeds, size is less of an issue in aging than with dog breeds, where it is a major factor. For example, compare the size of a Chihuahua versus a Great Dane; there is no comparable size difference in the cat species. That is not to say that size cannot affect a cat's health. It can, especially when it comes to weight. As in humans and dogs, overweight and obese cats are much more prone to certain diseases and shorter lifespan than cats kept at their proper weight. (More on weight below and in Chapter 5.)

World Record Holder

There are a number of contenders for oldest cat on record, but the *Guinness Book of World Records* cites as its winning entry the appropriately named Granpa, who lived to be thirty-four years, two months, and four hours. He died on April 1, 1998. His longevity did not go unnoticed before he died, either: Granpa was honored as the centerfold in the March 1997 issue of *Cat Fancy*.

Breed also can become an important factor in your cat's life expectancy if he is a purebred. Many cat lovers have a particular preference—some would say devotion—to a specific breed of cat, such as the Siamese or Persian. Both the short- and long-term health of purebred cats depends greatly on the breeder. Disreputable breeders often resort to the practice of inbreeding, the interbreeding of closely related individuals (e.g., mothers and sons, sisters and brothers, etc.) for the purpose of preserving and fixing desirable characteristics and/or to eliminate unfavorable characteristics, such as shape of ear, length of hair, coat color, and many others. Unfortunately, the practice also can result in heightened tendency to develop either behavioral or physical dysfunctions. (For example, purebreds such as the Himalayan, Persian, Siamese, Burmese, and Abyssinian seem to experience a higher incidence of periodontal [dental] disease.) As in dogs, mixed-breed cats have what's called "hybrid vigor," a well-balanced strength or force typical of crossbred animals (and plants, too, by the way).

Breed Right

For more on breeders and breeding, go to the Cat Fanciers' Association Web site, www.cfainc.org. Or, if you have a specific breed of cat, chances are there's an organization dedicated to it, where you will find breeder information and referrals.

The Environmental Effect

Where your cat lives also has a lot to do with how long he'll live. Is your cat a city feline, confined to an apartment? Is your cat a sub-urbanite, living indoors much of the time but with access to a yard, where he's free to prowl part of the day? Or is your cat a rural roamer, unconfined and outdoors most of the time? Dr. Barbara A. Kalvig, DVM, medical director for the New York Veterinary Hospital, says that environment is a major factor in how quickly and to what extent pet owners seek medical treatment for their cats. She sees a big difference between indoor cats, whose owners are more closely attuned to them (and, for example, see their cats' stools on a daily basis and note changes almost immediately), as opposed to suburban or rural cats who are just let out in the yard and not monitored as closely. In addition, environment is an issue when it comes to your cat's health care program. Outdoor cats, for example, are exposed to many more parasites and infections, and so may require more frequent vaccinations than their indoor counterparts.

Rural versus urban veterinary care also is part of the environmental equation. In general, urban pets may receive better care simply because pet owners in larger municipalities have access to the full range of veterinary specialists—including board-certified internists, surgeons, ophthalmologists, dermatologists, dentists, behaviorists, oncologists, holistic practitioners, and more. Rural communities generally cannot support this advanced level of care and technology.

Pet-Healthy Cities

When it comes to choosing where we live, most of us follow a job opportunity, a spouse, a climate, or a culture. If our pets could choose, they might follow their nose to one of the "pet-healthiest cities," as determined by a survey conducted in 2005 by the Purina Pet Institute's Healthy Pets 21 Consortium, in conjunction with demographic consultant Bert Sperling (who collects and analyzes the data for *Money* magazine's annual Best Places to Live). Using twenty-three criteria in three categories—health, services, and legislation—the institute compiled the first-ever list of the fifty healthiest cities for pets in the United States. The top five are:

1. Denver, Colorado
2. Minneapolis, Minnesota
3. Columbus, Ohio
4. Philadelphia, Pennsylvania
5. Seattle, Washington

What do these locales have that others don't? According to the consortium, they all scored high in meeting such criteria as high vet-to-pet ratios (Denver boasts one vet for every 1,200 pets), number of affiliated staff at accredited veterinary hospitals, number of veterinary surgeons, access to emergency veterinary care, number of certified shelters, and appropriate rabies vaccination and pet identification requirements, licensing fee reductions for spayed/neutered pets, and cruelty investigation programs.

Other cities making the list (and their rank) include San Francisco (8), Los Angeles (13), Boston (17), Chicago (18), New York City (35), Cincinnati (42), and Miami (50).

Nutrition: Taking Care of the Inner Cat

There's no question that what cats eat has a marked impact on their life expectancy and quality of life. Now, thanks to advances in research and a deeper understanding of how cats digest and process food, feeding a cat properly should be no problem. But it still can be. Why? Because in tandem with greater knowledge in the field of animal nutrition has come an almost mind-boggling range of pet foods. Trolling the aisles of your favorite pet supply or grocery store, you've no doubt been amazed—if not overwhelmed—by the myriad brands and types of cat food now on the shelves. In bags and boxes, cans and pouches, cartons and other distinctive containers, there's seemingly a flavor and diet suitable for cats of every size, shape, age, and physical condition. But are they as suitable as they promise? How do you know and how do you choose?

Just by asking those questions, you're on the right path to finding the appropriate food(s) for your senior cat. Now is the right time to reevaluate your cat's diet, in consultation with your vet and as part of his regular checkups. In Chapters 4 and 5 we'll talk more about cat food, and how to be sure your cat is on the right diet for his age and health status. For now, as noted above, keep in mind that overweight and obese cats have shorter life expectancies than those kept at or near their ideal weight. And animals maintained strictly on high-quality balanced commercial diets live longer than animals fed table scraps or cheaper brands of cat food, since high-fat and/or low-fiber diets decrease life expectancy. Sound familiar?

SUMMARY

It's never too late to start giving your older cat the care he needs, but sooner is definitely better. To that end, be alert to signs that changes are taking place in your cat's body and behavior, and address them promptly with your vet. The best chance your cat has for a long and healthy life depends on your attentiveness. In the next chapter, we begin by learning to read vital signs your cat may be sending you.

KEY PET POINTS

- As accurately as possible, estimate your cat's age, in cat years. If you don't know when he was born, ask your vet to help determine his age, based on a physical and dental exam.
- Recognize that your environment affects your cat's health as much as it does your own.
- It may be easier, more convenient, and less expensive to grab your grocery store's generic-brand cat food off the shelf. But do you know what's in there? It could, over time, seriously impact your cat's well-being.

CHAPTER 2

Prevention: Taking a Proactive Approach to Caring for Your Cat

Taking preventive measures for the care of your cat is the best way to ensure quality of life for her, for as long as possible. Even in the best-case scenario, the age-related changes your cat will inevitably experience may cause major disruptions in your life, on practical, psychological, and emotional levels. By being prepared, you stand the best chance of doing right by your cat—and yourself.

This chapter offers four guidelines that, taken together, can form an effective strategy for caring for your aging or geriatric cat:

1. Pay attention.
2. Schedule biannual checkups.
3. Plan ahead.
4. Trust your instincts.

PAY ATTENTION

As we all know from trying to multitask our way through our increasingly busy lives, rarely do we truly give anything the attention it deserves. So it's understandable if you find yourself being less than attentive to that bundle of fur curled up in the tangle of your bedclothes—especially since she sleeps sixteen to eighteen hours a day (lucky "dog"). And, as pointed out in Chapter 1, it goes against a cat's very nature to broadcast the fact that she's not feeling well or is starting to suffer age-related maladies. But she can, and will, give you signs. It's up to you to recognize them. You may not know exactly how to interpret these signs—that's what your cat's veterinarian is for—but unless you're paying attention, you'll pass them by on the way to grab another cup of coffee, and miss the first and best chance you have to give your cat the care she needs. Dr. Grace Bransford of the Ross Valley Veterinary Hospital in San Anselmo, California, says the biggest mistake pet owners make in caring for their cats is "not seeing." Not seeing comes from not paying attention.

To give you a head start on this important step, take a look at the checklist titled "Signs Your Cat Is Getting Old." Maybe you're already aware, if only vaguely, of some of these signs; if so, check them off as a way to bring attention to them. If nothing rings a bell yet, consider yourself lucky; but keep these signs in mind (better yet, make a copy of this list and keep it handy) so that you're prepared to make note of them and pass the information on to your vet. This list is by no means comprehensive, and every cat is different, so jot down anything and everything in your cat's behavior or demeanor that strikes you as "not right."

In Chapter 3, "Vital Signs: Recognizing Signals of Change from Your Cat," you'll learn more about what these and other signs might mean. For now just be aware that keeping a list like this up to date will be valuable down the road, for three important purposes:

- You will be better prepared to help your vet help your cat.
- You will have an easier time understanding the objectives of the screening exams your vet will conduct.
- You will more fully understand the reasoning behind treatments or lifestyle adjustments (including nutrition, exercise, and grooming) your vet may recommend for your cat.

And that leads us to the second guideline: taking your cat in for regular checkups.

Signs Your Cat Is Getting Old

Sign	Yes	No
Difficulty jumping up?		
Increased stiffness or limping?		
Change in litterbox habits?		
Increased thirst?		
Increased urination?		
Straining while defecating?		
Change in activity level?		
Change in breathing? Panting?		
Lapse in, or inadequate, grooming habits?		
Confusion or disorientation?		
Excessive crying/"talking" or change in tone?		
Lethargy? Hiding?		
Decreased responsiveness?		
Tremors or shaking?		
Skin or coat changes?		
Lumps or bumps on skin?		
Excessive scratching?		
Changes in sleeping patterns/locations?		
Change in demeanor? Increased irritability?		
Altered appetite?		
Weight change (up or down)?		
Vomiting, diarrhea, or constipation?		
Bad breath?		
Other?		

Source: Adapted with permission from William Fortney, DVM.

SCHEDULE BIANNUAL CHECKUPS

Even if you've noticed no signs so far that your cat is experiencing age-related health changes, that doesn't mean she isn't. Many, maybe most, are not apparent to the naked eye. That's why veterinarians are

Inside Information

If your cat spends part or most of her time outdoors, you will have a more difficult time tracking changes in your cat as she ages. To get the "inside information" you will need to ensure she stays healthy for the long term, you'll have to make an extra effort to tune in. A good time is when you feed her. Instead of just putting her food down and going about your business, stand by and watch; see if she's having trouble chewing, for example, or is drinking large quantities of water. You might also want to consider keeping her in at night, and installing a litter box indoors (if she doesn't have one already). The point is to give yourself opportunities to really "see" your cat.

---

unanimous in their conviction that biannual checkups for aging cats—beginning at the magic number seven—is the *single best way* to keep your cat well cared for throughout her senior and geriatric years. I know, I know: it's a miracle when you remember to schedule an appointment once a year for your own annual checkup. But, says Dr. Goldston, "No health care program is more important in maintaining and prolonging a high-quality life for the pet, while meeting the most important needs of the owner, than a thorough geriatrics wellness program that is carried out to the fullest." Note that he included meeting *your* needs, too: imagine your life without your cat. The years we have with them are too short as it is, and this is one small way to extend those years.

Sad to say, though, too many of us fail to take this important step. According to the AAHA's "Senior Care Guidelines," only some 14 percent of senior animals are taken for the checkups recommended by their veterinarians.

Why is this twice-a-year checkup so important to your cat? Three important reasons: first, it enables the early detection of abnormalities,

Top Priority

Though too few owners of older cats follow the twice-a-year checkup recommendation, overall most say they are more likely to take better care of their cats' health than they do their own. According to a pet owner survey conducted in 2004 by the AAHA, 58 percent of 1,238 pet owners surveyed in more than 160 accredited veterinary practices said they visit their pets' veterinarian more often than their own physician. More interesting still is that 93 percent said they are likely to risk their own lives for their pets.

which, second, makes it possible for your vet to design an individualized health care program for your cat; and third, it allows your vet to establish baseline data about your cat's health, which he or she will use subsequently to compare against information gathered at future checkups. According to the AAHA's "Senior Care Guidelines," "A wealth of scientific literature documents the presence of subclinical disease [meaning the disease is present but not yet causing external symptoms] in some healthy-appearing animals; to illuminate such conditions, there is no substitute for a thorough and complete history and physical examination. In addition, subtle changes in laboratory test results may give an indication of the presence of underlying disease." With early detection—and thanks to the numerous advances being made every day in veterinary medicine—it is often possible to postpone, or minimize, the effects of those changes, sometimes for years. Moreover, taking preventive measures may spare you costly treatments down the road. Isn't that worth taking out your calendar and scheduling two appointments now? As Dr. Goldston says, "This geriatric wellness program is good for our patients, it's good for our clients, and it's good for our hospitals."

Tip

If you celebrate your cat's birthday, what better way than to schedule one checkup on that date and the second six months afterward? Also, find out whether your vet sends out reminder cards, to help you follow through.

The Geriatric Wellness Program: The Short Version

My objective here is to give you an overview within the broader context of prevention. Chapter 4, "Wellness Programs: Keeping Your Cat Healthy for the Long Term," details the various components of a typical geriatric wellness workup.

Beginning when your cat enters her geriatric years, this program should continue through her "golden" years. For you, the program will involve discussions and decisions of medical treatments, terminal illness, and, eventually, death (natural or by euthanasia). Ideally, says Dr. Goldston, the program will also include the handling of your pet's remains, your grief process (including bereavement counseling), and, possibly, welcoming a new cat into your life. For your cat, the program will involve a number of elements. Briefly:

Physical exam: Includes a check of your cat's general appearance and all organ systems; temperature, pulse, and respiration (TPR); body weight; heart and lungs; ears, eyes, and teeth; thyroid glands; and skin.

Complete blood test: Helps to diagnose infection, anemia, bleeding problems, and cancer. Also gives insight into your cat's immune system.

Serum chemistry profile: Assesses function of liver, kidneys, pancreas, and other organs.

Complete urinalysis: Assesses kidney function and reveals infection.

Fecal analysis: Checks for evidence of parasites and unusual bacteria and protozoa; evaluates red and white blood cells.

On an individual basis, as necessary, your vet may recommend other tests, such as:

- Radiography
- Echocardiography
- Abdominal ultrasonography
- Thyroid and adrenal gland testing
- Blood pressure measurement
- Other organ function tests

What, you might ask, is the point of doing all these tests on an old cat? As stated previously, early detection enables more effective treatment. Even those diseases and disorders that are incurable from the outset can be controlled and managed, if major tissue or organ damage has not yet occurred, says Dr. Goldston. The bottom line for your cat: longer life, at a higher quality. The bottom line for you: more valuable time with your favorite lap warmer.

Test Preparation

Before doing any additional testing, your vet should explain to you the purpose of the test, why he or she thinks it is necessary (what, exactly, he or she is looking for), and how much it will cost. Your vet should ask you for permission to proceed with the additional work.

PLAN AHEAD

Everything we've been talking about so far could probably fall under this heading. But this section is intended specifically to address day-to-day life with a geriatric cat, for a great deal of what happens to an aging animal falls in the realm of the unexpected. Your cat probably will not start having seizures on the very day you have scheduled to take her to the vet. More likely, it will happen late on a Sunday afternoon, or when you're out of town on business and your cat is in the care of a pet sitter. Now what? These situations are never pleasant or easy, but how well you have planned for the unexpected will, to some degree, dictate the outcome. Here are some guidelines for making the best of a bad situation.

Prepare for Emergencies

No matter how conscientious you are, no matter how carefully you pay attention and take all the proper precautions, your geriatric cat is going to present you with some challenging, even daunting, moments. Few of us are at our best at such times; many of us become unglued, especially when a loved one is in danger or pain. To ensure that cooler heads prevail when your cat is in trouble, take these precautions:

1. **Have names and numbers handy.** Post them on the refrigerator, on the side of the computer monitor, or wherever your go-to spot is in your home. The names and numbers you should include are those for:

- Your veterinarian
- The nearest emergency services veterinary hospital or clinic (preferably a twenty-four-hour facility)
- Poison control center or hotline

Be sure to add the number for the ASPCA Animal Poison Control Center, in Urbana, Illinois, to your emergency call list: 888-426-4435. The ASPCA Poison Control Center is staffed by veterinary toxicologists. Grab your credit card before you call, as there's a consultation fee—around $50.

Help! My Cat Just Ate Something . . .

Cats are notorious for eating plants and other substances they shouldn't. Securely seal and store household cleaners, insecticides, and rodenticides. Familiarize yourself with plants (especially indoor) that may be hazardous to your cat's health. The AVMA Web site (www.avma.org) has "A Pet Owner's Guide to Poisons," as does the Web site for Maine Coon Rescue (http://mainecoonrescue.com/poison.html).

---

2. **Keep your cat's medical paperwork handy.** Maintain a file of your cat's vaccinations, medications, and other medical records; keep it up to date and easily accessible. In an emergency, remember, you may not be seeing your cat's regular vet, and you'll want to provide the emergency practitioner with as much background information as possible.
3. **Learn some basic first-aid/emergency procedures.** You may find yourself in the unenviable position of having to act now and call for help later. Maybe your cat is choking or bleeding. Knowing basic first aid could save your cat's life. It's a good idea to purchase one of the numerous first-aid books

Caution

If you have to administer emergency first aid to your cat, as soon as possible thereafter, take her to a veterinarian for follow-up care—even if your cat seems past the crisis. Only a vet can confirm that all is well.

for cats that are now available. Ask your vet to recommend a good one—and to step through the procedures with you, if you are not comfortable performing first aid on your cat. To get an idea of what such books contain, go online and check out *First Aid: Emergency Care for Dogs and Cats* (by Roger W. Gfeller, DVM, and Michael W. Thomas, DVM; with Isaac Mayo). It is available for browsing at www.veterinarypartner.com. You might also want to call your local animal shelter or humane organization to find out if a first-aid training program for pets is offered in your community.

4. **Assemble a first-aid kit.** Use a toolbox, a sewing box, or any other container that can conveniently store the following supplies:

- Cotton—rolled and in balls
- Gauze pads and medical paper tape
- Nonstick bandages
- Scissors, tweezers, and nail clippers
- Muzzle—actual or makeshift, such as strips of cotton, to prevent biting
- Latex gloves
- Towels or pillowcase, to restrain cat for treatment
- Wet wipes
- Sterile saline solution and ear-cleaning solution
- Hydrogen peroxide

- Plastic eyedropper or syringe
- Ice pack
- Rectal thermometer
- Pet carrier

You might want to add copies of your emergency phone list and your cat's medical file to the kit, too.

Just as important is what *not* to include in your kit, and primarily that means drugs. Drug poisoning, reports the American Veterinary Medical Association (AVMA), is the most common cause of poisoning in small animals. You should contact a veterinarian before giving your cat *any* medication, because even if it is safe in some doses, it may not be safe for a cat to ingest a human dose. For example, acetaminophen (e.g., Tylenol) tablets are highly toxic to cats. Cats are also highly sensitive to nonsteroidal anti-inflammatory drugs (NSAIDs) found in most pet owners' medicine cabinets—aspirin, ibuprofen (e.g., Advil and Nuprin), and naproxen. And *never* give a dog's medication to your cat.

5. Include other caregivers in your plans. Do you use the services of a pet sitter or a boarding facility? Give anyone and everyone who comes in regular contact with your cat and is responsible for her care at any time the list of contact numbers you compiled, along with a copy of your cat's medical file. Write

---

First Aid to Go

Instead of assembling your own, you can get ready-made first-aid kits for pets, such as one from CPR Savers & First Aid Supply, which offers wholesale kits of all kinds. The Web site is www.cpr-savers.com.

---

down where you can be reached at all times. And whenever you will be out of town, supply a secondary local contact name and number; this should be someone who knows you well and whom you trust to act on your behalf in your absence.

Spay/Neuter: Better Late Than Never

Ideally, your cat was spayed or neutered as a youngster. But if not, did you know that doing so is one of the best preventive measures you can take to reduce the risk of serious illness in senior cats? Many owners of older pets are afraid to submit them to this procedure; but vets agree, it's much less dangerous to have older cats spayed or neutered than to have them undergo treatment for reproductive organ diseases, certain cancers, and other diseases more prevalent in "intact" cats.

Of course, for an older cat, more precautions are necessary, and your veterinarian will have to conduct a thorough exam and run bloodwork and other tests before performing the procedure. But unless your cat is very old or in poor medical condition, spaying or neutering is still generally advisable.

Senior-Sensitize Your Home

One of the kindest and most effective preventive measures you can take for your senior pet's benefit is to adjust your cat's environment, based on her needs. For example:

1. If your cat has arthritis or other joint/muscle problems, and your house is large and/or has stairs, place additional water bowls and litter boxes strategically and conveniently so that your cat can easily access them at all times. (Don't forget to freshen the water and clean those auxiliary "comfort stations" at least once a day.)
2. If your cat has mobility or sensory loss problems of any kind

and is having difficulty getting up on your bed or other furniture, give her a step up, with a portable ramp or steps to make her access easier. Both are readily available from such pet supply companies as Doctors Foster & Smith (800-381-7179; www.drsfostersmith.com) or Senior Pet Products (800-805-2001; www.senior pet products.com).

3. If your cat has hearing or vision loss, minimize stress caused by those disabilities by putting her bed(s) in quiet, low-traffic areas of your home.
4. If your cat has become temperature sensitive—especially to cold (common among cats with chronic kidney disease)—consider treating her to thermal bedding. Several safe varieties are available from most cat supply catalogs and pet superstores.
5. Consider replacing high-sided litter boxes with those that offer easier access (either with low sides or a ramp), to prevent accidents from happening.

These are just a few suggestions; most people find very creative, innovative, and inexpensive (i.e., do-it-yourself) ways to accommodate their cat's disabilities, which are in many cases "suggested" by their cat's behavior. And don't give up if one solution doesn't pan out. Keep trying: you'll find what works best for you and your cat.

Tune In to Pet Care

Marty Becker, DVM, co-author of the fastest-selling pet book in history, *Chicken Soup for the Pet Lover's Soul,* and veterinary contributor to ABC's *Good Morning America,* now hosts a weekly radio program, "Top Vets Talk Pets," live at 10 a.m. EST on the Health Radio Network. On the one-hour program, Dr. Becker discusses pet health issues and takes listener calls. At the time of this writing, the program, which has the support of the American Animal Hospital Association (AAHA), was being broadcast in just a few U.S. markets, but you can listen in at www.healthradionetwork.com.

Raise Social Awareness

Like many geriatric humans, older cats, too, can become more irritable as they age. Hearing or vision loss causes them to be more easily startled or scared, and they may react by hissing or scratching, though more likely they'll just become more reclusive. Skin irritations can make them more sensitive to touch, especially the sometimes unintentionally rough handling from children. Joint and muscle aches make them (more) stubborn and crabby; they don't like to move from their favorite spots, no matter how inconvenient they may be for their human companions.

It's also important to be aware that older cats don't like changes in their routine and environment, so you'll need to be particularly vigilant when making any alterations. If, say, you are bringing home a new baby or another pet, plan in advance how you intend to introduce your old cat to what she may regard as the "interloper." You might want to call on the services of a behavior counselor to guide you through this period. Your vet or local humane organization can recommend a counselor for you; or go to the Association of Companion Animal Behavior Counselors' (ACABC) Web site, http://animalbehaviorcounselors.org, and click on "Find a Counselor or Member."

THE STORY OF FELIX AND MAX: PERIOD OF ADJUSTMENT

Adjusting to change: it's more difficult for some than others, cats included. In the case of Felix and Max, who share similar backgrounds, they couldn't have reacted more differently when brought together to share a household.

Felix, already an adult and grossly overweight, was left behind when his owners moved out of their small-town apartment. Like a piece of furniture that "would not do," he was set out on the curb, perhaps in hopes that, like a chair or chest of drawers, someone would find a place for him in their home. Fortunately, that's exactly what happened, though it took a while before anyone realized his former owners had gone and that Felix had been left to fend for himself. When it became clear what had happened, a cat-loving English teacher in town soon scooped up the black-and-white heavyweight, had him checked out by the local vet, put him on a strict diet, and gave him the run of a lovely apartment not too far from his old home. He had a cat's-eye view of the goings-on in town, through floor-to-ceiling windows in the living room, a basketful of toys, and a share in the nice large bed upstairs.

Max, on the other hand, was approximately only forty-five days old when he was found—or more precisely, heard, for it was his tiny voice that captured the attention of an architect on his way to work one morning. It took a while for him to realize that the voice was coming from under the hood of a parked car. It took another while to find the owner of the car, who opened the hood to reveal a tiny, half-starved kitten who had clearly gone in to warm himself by the heat of the engine. It was doubtful at first that he would survive, but slowly and surely Max made a successful recovery (which included surgery on one paw, to repair joint damage). During his recuperation, Max and the architect became inseparable, and Max grew into his lovely Siamese coat in high style.

Some five years later, the teacher and the architect, who had become friends, decided to share an apartment, and they agreed it would be the teacher's much

Felix (left) and Max: The feline art of coexistence

larger place. Felix was now an older cat, and very set in his ways; Max, too, was an adult, and used to having things his own way, for he had been spoiled outrageously. So it was that the teacher and the architect worried less about merging their belongings and more about merging their cats.

In preparation for the big day, the architect consulted his vet about the best way to introduce "the boys" to each other. The vet told him that the fact that both cats had been neutered gave them a leg up on the process, but that there would be, nevertheless, a period of adjustment—which would inevitably include some "disagreements." He also suggested the first face-to-face meeting of the cats be through the mesh windows of their cat carriers.

Remarkably, the first three weeks went fairly smoothly, all things considered. There were some minor daytime confrontations and a few hissing and spitting matches in the middle of the night, but overall, Felix and Max seemed to be adjusting to sharing space with each other. Max even tried to engage Felix in some typical cat shenanigans. And though Felix couldn't be bothered to humor the "kid," he didn't seem particularly put off by the younger cat's attempts to make friends.

But then, at about the fourth week, Felix's demeanor began to change noticeably. He seemed despondent—there was no other word for it. And though the apartment had been his home for several years now, he seemed to be deferring to the newcomer, and skulked around as if he didn't belong. He no longer slept in his owner's bed, but stayed downstairs by himself. And he became cranky—sensitive to touch and to being approached in general.

And after a successful weight-loss program that had made him a whole new cat, Felix had begun stealing Max's food—his way, perhaps, of reclaiming his territory.

Why? Felix has been given a clean bill of health physically, so is he having a more difficult time because he's older? Or is it because he was already an adult when he was abandoned, and can't "get over it"? Is Max more secure because he was rescued in infancy and has known only protective, loving care his whole life? These questions remain unanswered, because no one can fully know the psyche of the cat. But there can be no doubt that age plays a role here, and that stress over time, particularly for an older cat, can impact health just as it can in humans.

There is no end to this story, for Max and Felix and their owners are still trying to work things out. Fortunately for the boys, their owners are paying close attention to the behavior of both of them during this critical adjustment period, and do not hesitate to consult with experts, to help them chart this sometimes rocky path.

TRUST YOUR INSTINCTS

Access to the best-educated and best-trained veterinarians and the most advanced medical technologies and treatments is meaningless without you. Without your intimate knowledge and understanding of your cat, the "best" provider or medication is just something to read about in professional publications and marketing materials. In other words, you have to get in touch with that knowledge, and *trust* it. Don't push aside "funny feelings," "gut sensations," or "hunches" when it comes to your cat. Dr. Barbara Kalvig says it's surprising how many people bring in their pets because "they just have a feeling" something might be wrong—and usually they're right! Often, she says, it's nothing they can even put their finger on, such as one of the signs of aging listed on page 27. It's more a vague awareness they feel compelled to follow up on.

What's going on here? Mental telepathy or just proof of the extraordinary bond you share with your cat? That's for you to decide; it doesn't really matter whether you attribute such "insider information" to the mystical or the more down to earth. What matters is that you act on it. What have you got to lose: a little time and the cost of a visit to your vet? Small price to pay for peace of mind.

I Hear What You're Saying: Animal Communicators

A growing number of pet owners are calling on the services of *animal communicators*, who believe it is possible to *exchange* information with animals, most commonly between one person and his or her pet. Typically, the communicator transmits questions to and from the pet and the person telepathically—words may not be spoken aloud, and the communicator and the animal need not even be in the same location (communicators often work by phone and e-mail). Usually, the communicator then "translates" the pet's messages into human language.

Frequent issues raised by clients of animal communicators include: behavior problems, understanding an animal's needs and feelings, working with veterinarians, locating lost animals, learning when an animal is ready to die, and communicating with a pet after it has died.

If this is an avenue you want to pursue as part of your cat's health care program, be sure to get recommendations for a communicator. Most vets can give you either a direct referral or the name of a client who uses one. And be aware that costs vary widely, anywhere from $25/hour to $300/hour.

SUMMARY

An ounce of prevention still is worth a pound of cure—although where an aging cat's health is concerned, that may be an undervaluation. By taking a proactive stance regarding your cat's health care, you are in the best position to act and react conscientiously and with love, no matter what the circumstance. You'll also be better able to read the vital signs your cat may send, which are discussed in the next chapter.

KEY PET POINTS

- You love your cat, of course, but even the most devoted pet owner may, in the course of a busy life, start to take things for granted. Your cat's long-term health depends on your paying attention to the changes she'll be going through as she ages.
- Don't wait until something's wrong to call your vet. Do it now: schedule two appointments, six months apart.
- Expect the best, but plan for the worst. Old cats are more prone to accidents and sudden illness. Prepare for emergencies: know who you're going to call, where you're going to go, and what you're going to do until you can reach help.
- You know your cat better than anyone else, including your vet. Trust that knowledge and act on it whenever you think you should.

CHAPTER 3

Vital Signs: Recognizing Signals of Change from Your Cat

Even the most devoted of cat lovers, if they are being honest, will admit it's not possible to ever really know a cat. Cats are masters of mystery. That's not to say, however, that they can't communicate with us. On the contrary. Anyone who has ever been on the receiving end of a glare from a cat who doesn't like what he's been served for dinner has understood the message perfectly. Similarly, one has only to look at a cat basking in the sun, eyes open to only the narrowest of slits, tail softly twitching, to know that he is content. And what cat lover hasn't seen the look of disdain on a feline's face when, say, in the presence of a dog begging for attention—the look that says, "I would never stoop to such behavior."

But when it comes to expressing physical and mental discomfort, cats typically leave their owners totally clueless, for they retain a self-protective instinct from their wilder days to hide weakness from predators. But humans are tuned to a different frequency, one that best understands clear, vocal expressions of discomfort. Unless and until they're in extreme pain, at which point they may howl or merely raise the volume on their usual tone, cats often "say" nothing to alert us to their distress.

Purr-fect Disguise

Is there any sound on earth more soothing than the purr of a cat? People have always assumed that cats purr as an indication that they are happy or content. But, in fact, cats also purr when they're under duress and in pain, some even when they're dying. The fact that they do this, and the frequency range (between 25 and 150 hertz) and pattern (both when they inhale and exhale), has led some scientists to conclude that the sound frequencies of this distinctive vocalization may improve bone density and improve healing.

What you as a cat owner must realize is that purring is not necessarily a sign that all is well. You must pay close attention to the other signs described in Chapter 2 and in this chapter to ensure you're "reading" your cat accurately.

More outward signs of aging probably may be readily apparent to you: increased irritability; decreased energy; altered sleep patterns and a change in eating habits and/or appetite; or weight loss. But some will come on so gradually they might slip by you, or you might be tempted to "write them off" as due to old age. But remember what Dr. Goldston said is the most common mistake people make in evaluating the health of their aging cats: interpreting signs of change as "just getting old" and failing to get them checked out.

Changes associated with the process of aging often are indicators of a developing or existing problem, which, left untreated, can impact your cat's life—and your life with him. That's why these are considered vital signs—they're fundamental clues to your cat's health, hence his quality of life and life expectancy. That's not to say that your cat now has, or will in the future have, the diseases or disorders associated with the changes described below. The objective of this chapter is not to alarm you. Don't, for example, automatically assume the worst of the associated diseases/disorders/conditions listed in each category (for example, not every lump is a cancer). Nor is it to suggest that you should diagnose based on these signs—in fact, that's the last thing you should do. The goal here is to alert you to common age-related changes and to inform you as to possible causes, so that you can keep track and inform your vet at your cat's next checkup—or sooner if the sign is more serious. It's his or her job to determine what, if anything, is wrong and to inform you of what you can and should do about it.

BODY PARTS AND FUNCTIONS

This section describes how each part of your cat's body might break down as he ages, to give you a more thorough understanding of the signs of your cat's physical aging process.

Note

Many of the most prevalent diseases and disorders associated with these changes are covered in Chapter 6.

Metabolism

We humans tend to think of our metabolism primarily as the villain we fight in the battle against weight gain. We envy those people with "high metabolism," who never seem to gain a pound, and we cite our slowing metabolism as the reason we can't seem to lose weight no matter what we do and what we eat, particularly as we grow older.

Metabolism slows with aging in cats, too, so you may have noticed that yours is starting to gain weight—especially if you've been feeding him essentially the same diet since he was a young adult and he's getting less exercise than he used to. In extreme cases, the result is obesity, which, as in the human population, has become a major precursor of serious disease in cats. A decreased metabolic rate, plus lack of activity, reduces caloric need between 30 to 40 percent. That means you probably need to start feeding your cat different food (details on that in Chapter 5, "Keeping Your Cat in Shape: Nutrition, Exercise, and Grooming").

Obesity: Battle of the Bulge

Obesity is bigger than a sign; it's a billboard, one that reads in supersized, boldface letters: "Overweight cats at greater risk." Why then do so many cat owners miss or ignore it? Simply because weight, like beauty, seems to be in the eye of the beholder. According to vets from around the country, many pet owners whose cats are overweight or obese see their cats' weight as normal, or correct, for their size; furthermore, they often think that an appropriate weight looks too thin, or unhealthy.

As a cat owner, in addition to knowing how much your cat weighs, you need to understand what's referred to as "body condition." This gives a much clearer indication of whether or not your cat needs to lose weight, as it describes not only how your cat should look, but also *feel* to you. For example, on an ideal-weight cat, you should be able to easily feel his ribs through his coat, but not see them sticking out. His abdomen should also have a visible "tuck" when viewed from the side. (Chapter 5 has more on the threat of obesity to your cat's health.)

An even more important metabolic message in cats is weight loss, especially if it is dramatic—seemingly overnight—and without a change in eating habits (i.e., your cat still has a good appetite). Don't wait for your cat to get bone-thin to take him to the vet. There are a number of possible causes, including hyperthyroidism (overactive thyroid disease), the most common hormonal disorder in aging cats.

Signs: weight gain or loss; change in or loss of appetite

Associated diseases/disorders/conditions: weight gain—heart disease, hypertension, arthritis; weight loss—hyperthyroidism, metabolic disorders (i.e., kidney, liver, or gastrointestinal disease), oral or dental disease, diabetes mellitus

Muscles, Bones, and Joints

Just like us, as cats age, they lose muscle tone and bone and cartilage mass. The common results: joint stiffness, arthritis, brittle bones, and muscle weakness. Overall, your cat will become less flexible, less active, and perhaps show signs of weakness or lethargy.

Signs: limping; difficulty jumping up and down; sensitivity to cold; greater irritability and less interest in activity; lapse in grooming

Associated diseases/disorders/conditions: arthritis, obesity

Skin, Hair, and Nails

An older cat's skin becomes dry and thin and loses elasticity, making it more prone to irritation and infection. Lumps and bumps on and under the skin also are common to the aging cat.

He will be less conscientious about grooming (sometimes due to other physical ailments such as arthritis or obesity), resulting in hair matting (especially in long-haired cats), dandruff, odor, and other skin conditions. His claws will become more brittle, thicker, and overgrown (sometimes curling around into the footpad). Older cats also have greater difficulty retracting their claws, and this can literally trip them up, when they get caught in any fiber, carpeting in particular.

Signs: nonstop scratching; skin flaking or dandruff; body odor; hair loss or matting; weird growths or skin discoloration

Associated diseases/disorders/conditions: obesity; parasite invasion; cancer or benign tumors

Eyes

One of the signs in aging cats that owners notice first is a change in the appearance of their cat's eyes, most commonly described as "filmy" or "cloudy." Though this effect may seem to be a sign of impaired vision, it isn't always; often it is an indication of what's called *nuclear sclerosis*, a normal age-related change to the lens of the eye, which can, however, make it difficult for your cat to see at night or to focus close up.

Aging cats also can suffer more serious eye diseases, cataracts in particular. (Cats also get glaucoma, though they are far less prone to it than dogs.) Note that the aforementioned whiteness or cloudiness associated with nuclear sclerosis may also be a sign of cataracts, so always have this sign checked out by your vet. An aging cat's eyes may also suffer damage caused by hypertension (high blood pressure).

Signs: a white or bluish, milky look to the lenses; patchy look to the irises, which were formerly solid eye color; mucus buildup in the eye and/or discharge

Associated diseases/disorders/conditions: hypertension; nuclear sclerosis; cataracts; conjunctivitis; dry eye

Ears

Like elderly people, it's not uncommon for old cats to lose their hearing, either partially or entirely. This can cause them to become stressed, resulting in behavior changes such as increased irritability, reclusiveness, and a greater tendency to be startled by sudden movements, unexpected touch, and other changes. If your cat is allowed outdoors, it may be time to consider keeping him indoors permanently, or at least limiting his access and keeping an eye on him when he is allowed outside.

Be on the lookout, too, for any unusual discharge from your cat's ears—in particular when it's associated with an unpleasant odor, which often is a sign of an ear infection. As cats age they become more susceptible to parasites.

Signs: hearing loss—failure to respond normally to your voice, sounds, or other vocal stimuli; yowling incessantly; infection or parasites—constant scratching around the ears, with accompanying irritation and smelly, excessive discharge
Associated diseases/disorders/conditions: hearing loss/deafness; ear infection; parasite invasion

Nose and Throat

Dripping nose, sneezing, and coughing: sound like the common cold? Well, a cold's nothing to sneeze at in an older cat, as it might—especially if it persists—lead to much more serious, secondary infections. Cats really don't get colds, per se; instead, they get upper respiratory infections (URIs), which are highly contagious (either airborne or by contact) among cats. (Note: You cannot catch a cold from your cat, or vice versa.) Older cats in particular are susceptible to URIs due to weakened immune systems, as are cats that come into contact with other cats (e.g., they are free to roam the neighborhood, are boarded in kennels, or live in multicat households).

Generally, a URI is not serious and is easy to treat when addressed early; otherwise, it can lead to more serious problems.

Signs: runny nose; persistent sneezing and coughing; difficulty breathing; lack of energy; loss of appetite; discharge from eyes, nose, and/or mouth; oral ulcers

Associated diseases/disorders/conditions: cold; pneumonia; heart disease; heartworm; cancer

---

Nose for Food

Cats with an upper respiratory infection may stop eating because their sense of smell is impaired (they get "stuffed up" just like we do)—what they can't smell, they won't eat. And they can begin to lose weight quickly, putting them at greater risk for complications. In geriatric cats, a common cold can become uncommonly difficult to treat if not addressed early. A sneeze or two is probably no cause for alarm, but when accompanied by any of the other signs listed above, it's time to see a veterinarian.

Mouth

Do you brush your cat's teeth and gums regularly? If you do, you're in the minority of pet owners, and you're taking one of the most important steps to ensuring your cat's long life and good health. Many people are surprised to learn that good dental hygiene is one of the most crucial aspects of wellness in cats. It's about much, much more than bad breath and yellowing teeth. According to one report, 85 percent of cats (and dogs) four years and older suffer from periodontal disease, which left untreated can lead to infection of major organs such as the lungs, kidneys, and liver—even the nervous system—and, eventually, to death. The American Veterinary Dental College (AVDC) says periodontal disease is the most common clinical condition in companion animals. The good news is, periodontal disease is treatable in the early stages.

You'll also want to be on the lookout for any changes to the healthy pink color of your cat's gums, which can signal other problems, such as anemia (pale pink/almost-white gums).

Who's Who in Pet Health Care: American Veterinary Dental College (AVDC)

The AVDC, founded in 1988, is the clinical specialist organization for veterinary dentists. It is accredited by the American Board of Veterinary Specialties of the American Veterinary Medical Association (AVMA). The college is also involved in the prevention of oral disease through its sponsorship of the Veterinary Oral Health Council. Though primarily for professionals, you can learn a lot about companion animal dental care by going to www.avdc.org and clicking on the "Pet Owners" link.

Signs: bad breath; bleeding from the mouth; loose or discolored teeth; trouble eating/chewing, or dropping food; drooling; loss of appetite; sensitivity to touch around mouth area; change in gum color; oral ulcers

Associated diseases/disorders/conditions: gingivitis or periodontal disease; infection of major organs; oral cancers

Heart

Heart disease in cats can be very dangerous, because typically symptoms don't appear until the disease has progressed to the serious stage; or they mimic signs of other problems and so go untreated. Heart problems in felines usually take the form of cardiomyopathies, diseases of the heart muscle. The most common is hypertrophic cardiomyopathy, where areas of the heart muscle (usually the left ventricle) enlarge and thicken.

Signs: difficulty breathing, even at rest; loss of appetite and weight; intolerance to any exercise; lethargy, even fainting/collapsing; increased heart rate; leg paralysis

Associated diseases/disorders/conditions: cardiomyopathies; heartworm; arrhythmia

Liver

A cat's liver is one of the largest and most important organs in his body, processing nutrients and blood for use by the rest of his body. It's also one of the most amazing organs in that it has both a reserve and regeneration capacity. Unfortunately, it's that self-healing capability that means liver disease can go undetected until the liver is 70 to 80 percent damaged. Another good reason to take your aging cat for biannual checkups.

Signs: loss of appetite or weight loss: yellowing of skin, gums, and whites of eyes; vomiting and/or diarrhea; lethargy or irritability; seizures

Associated diseases/disorders/conditions: liver disease; parasite invasion; bacterial infection of the liver; infectious disease

Kidneys and Urinary Tract

The job of a cat's kidneys is manifold: they filter toxins and waste products from the blood and eliminate them, by way of the bladder, through urination; regulate electrolytes; produce an enzyme that helps regulate blood pressure (hypertension is common in aging cats); and manufacture a hormone that stimulates the production of red blood cells. So it is not surprising that when the kidneys fail to

THE STORY OF CHESSIE: SYMPTOMS OF CHANGE

Like so many cat-human "romances," Chessie's was one of serendipity. Found with a sibling (who later disappeared) near a children's shelter in Cambridge, Maryland, she was brought home by a kind-hearted area resident who happened to be hosting a couple from New Jersey. The husband immediately fell in love with the kitten, later estimated by a veterinarian to be around six months old. So Chessie, who was named after the mascot for the Chesapeake and Ohio Railroad, in short order, became a Jersey girl.

On the record as a smoke-colored domestic shorthair, Chessie often was mistaken for a Russian Blue by strangers. She didn't much care for strangers anyway, so what others thought hardly mattered. She reserved the warm and loving side of her nature for John and Maureen, who had given her a fresh start. What mattered was that she got to spend most days with John, a poet, who was ideal company for a cat; and she soon developed a rather cultured nature herself.

Life for Chessie wasn't all sun-filled window ledges and poetic musings on the passing birdlife, however. For within the first year in her new home, and after she was spayed, Chessie began showing all the classic symptoms of a urinary tract infection (UTI): howling, a nearly constant urge to urinate, coupled with diminished urinary output. UTIs became an almost annual event for Chessie. And the standard treatment—a course of antibiotics—proved to be a horrible experience for both Chessie and her owners, for she wouldn't "pill," foaming at the mouth and, at one point, becoming anorexic because she came to associate pills with food. This meant trips to the vet (which Chessie also hated) for injections of antibiotics. Relief would come when Chessie was nine years old, when the pet food manufacturer Hill's Pet Nutrition, Inc., began to market its cd/sd combination, described as a miracle for treating urinary tract infections. And for Chessie and her owners it was nothing short of that.

Chessie: A Jersey girl with poetic tendencies

Then, within months after going on the Hill's diet, Chessie started urinating copious amounts, often soaking her litter pan—which probably was the reason she also began to urinate elsewhere in the house. Because she had just gone on medicated food for the UTIs, Maureen and John attributed the increased urination to the new diet. But Chessie had also begun drinking large quantities of water—"like a dog," said Maureen. Due for a checkup anyway, Chessie was diagnosed with Type I diabetes (not enough insulin). Given the choice between a regimen of shots or special diet of food for diabetic cats, Maureen and John opted for shots, so they could keep Chessie on the cd/sd regimen to keep the UTIs at bay. And the combination of treatments seemed to work, for Chessie had three happy UTI-free years and never had a problem with either the prescription diet or the insulin injections. Maureen and John also were careful to maintain the proper amount of food Chessie was eating, as instructed by the veterinarian, in conjunction with her daily injections—though she was given a bit of fresh turkey or chicken on special occasions, but always in carefully monitored portion sizes.

It was shortly before Chessie's thirteenth birthday that Maureen began to notice Chessie wasn't eating as much and, one morning, seemed disoriented—"just not herself." Sadly, though, coping as they were at the same time with the loss of a close family member, Maureen and John delayed taking Chessie to the vet. They hoped her appetite would pick up and she would seem more like her normal self. By the time Maureen took her in, two or three weeks later, Chessie's metabolism was way off and she was very weak. And while at the vet's for testing, Chessie went into cardiac arrest and died.

Saying she'll "regret for the rest of her life" waiting to take Chessie to the vet when she began showing signs of deterioration, Maureen learned another important lesson about caring for a senior cat: becoming fully informed and being "persistent in getting our questions answered." Chessie's veterinarian, though caring and compassionate, was running a busy practice alone at the time of Chessie's initial diagnosis as a diabetic and failed to mention the importance of regular urine testing for diabetic cats until a couple of years later.

Maureen and John's new cat, Cholmondeley, is the beneficiary of their increased knowledge and understanding of feline health care.

function properly, a cat's health begins to suffer. But what is surprising to many cat lovers is that, in spite of its seriousness, the symptoms of kidney disease (commonly referred to as chronic renal failure, or CRF) are so subtle they can be overlooked until a great deal of damage has already been done—when kidney function has been reduced by as much as 70 percent.

Because the kidneys are part of the urinary tract, urinary tract infections (UTIs) have some of the same symptoms as kidney disease. But UTIs are much easier to treat, usually with a regimen of antibiotics. Your vet will have to run blood tests and take urine specimens to determine which your cat has.

Signs: increased, sometimes insatiable, thirst; frequent need to urinate (though, in the case of a UTI, with very little urine as a result); incontinence; blood in urine; loss of appetite

Associated diseases/disorders/conditions: chronic renal failure; urinary tract infection; diabetes mellitus

Digestive and Elimination Systems

A senior cat's digestive system can seem a study in contrasts. One cat may lose all interest in eating (perhaps because of a diminished sense of smell and taste) and start to lose weight, while another may seem interested in nothing but eating, and begin packing on the pounds. Either way, chances are neither is getting the nutrition he needs from his food, because the aging cat's digestive system loses the ability to absorb nutrients. Proper nutrition, a vital factor in maintaining your cat's health, is covered in Chapter 5, "Keeping Your Cat in Shape: Nutrition, Exercise, and Grooming." For now, recognize that your cat's interest—or lack thereof—in food may be a sign of other problems, so always bring changes in appetite and weight to the attention of your vet.

The Meat of the Matter

A very important fact to know about cats is that they are *carnivores.* That means they *must* eat meat in some form to survive. They have simple stomachs made to digest meat, and lack salivary amylase, an enzyme needed to break down plant matter. Dogs, by contrast, are considered *omnivores*; though by nature meat eaters, they can survive on plant material alone. Cats cannot.

As your cat ages he may also have more trouble keeping his food down. Vomiting occasionally is not uncommon and usually is not a sign of anything more serious than a hairball, an upset stomach, or that it's time to change his diet to one more tolerable to his more sensitive digestive system. But persistent vomiting is grave cause for concern, especially if there's blood or other foreign material in it. Likewise, retching—the action of vomiting, but with nothing to show for it—is serious business.

Doodie Duty

As a pet owner, it's not the most pleasant task in the world, to be sure, but it's an important one when it comes to caring for your aging cat: paying attention, on a regular basis, to the color and consistency of your cat's stool. And at some point, your vet will ask you to provide a stool sample as part of your cat's wellness workup. This will be easier for indoor cat owners, whose pets use litter pans. If your cat typically uses an "outhouse" and you've been asked to collect a stool sample, set up a litter box inside and don't let your cat out until he's provided what you need.

You may notice a similar set of contrasts in your cat's elimination system: he may have diarrhea or constipation; or he may suffer both from time to time. When either is short lived, it's probably nothing to worry about; but if your cat regularly suffers from one or both, or for more than a day or two, it's time to check with your vet. In the case of diarrhea, your cat can quickly become dehydrated, a serious condition; and prolonged constipation can be the sign of an intestinal blockage or tumor.

Signs: over-/undereating; vomiting or retching; diarrhea or constipation

Associated diseases/disorders/conditions: gastrointestinal disease; inflammatory bowel disease; kidney or liver disease; diabetes; cancer; reaction to medications

---

Cat Watch: Illness Indicators

- **Respiration:** Pay attention to prolonged coughing, sneezing, runny nose, or panting.
- **Mobility:** Note any difficulty climbing stairs, jumping up, or rising from and lowering to a resting position; limping or any change in gait; disorientation, loss of balance, or sudden collapses.
- **Coat and skin:** Watch for lumps and bumps, bald spots, and excessive shedding; monitor any sores for healing; note changes in grooming habits, resulting in matting, skin irritation, or odor; keep nails clipped.
- **Eyes, ears, and nose:** Be alert to repetitive or continual head shaking or pawing/scratching of head and ears; note any discharge or bad odor from ears. Monitor closely any discharge (especially thick and discolored) from eyes and nose.
- **Teeth and gums:** Pay attention to persistent bad breath, pale or yellow gums, tooth loss, or bleeding from mouth.
- **Appetite and eating:** Note both increased/decreased food/water consumption. Also note any new preferences—for canned food

over dry, for example. Watch for signs of difficulty chewing and/or swallowing. Also monitor refusal to eat, or "picky" eating, for more than one or two meals.

- **Weight:** Gains or losses can be gradual, so it's a good idea to weigh your older cat on a regular basis—say, every two months. Bring any sudden and dramatic changes (especially weight loss) to the attention of your vet immediately.
- **Elimination:** Monitor changes in color, consistency, and amount of stool and urine. Keep an eye out for blood in both stool and urine and for signs of pain while urinating/defecating. Note, too, changes in litter box habits.
- **Behavior:** Tune into personality changes, such as increased irritability, anxiety, or vocalizations; also watch for differences in sleep patterns and other behaviors.
- **Other illness indicators:** Bleeding from any part of the body; prolonged vomiting; sitting with head hanging over the water bowl but not drinking; swellings on the face, legs, or tail.

Brains and Behavior

Have you been wondering lately whether your cat's mind—you should excuse the expression—is "going to the dogs" these days? Has his behavior changed dramatically, and in a very short period of time? Does he fail to recognize you or others in your household? Does he seem lost or confused in his own home or other familiar surroundings? Does he pace or sit up all night instead of sleeping? Has his tone of voice changed or increased in volume? Does he howl ceaselessly, or repeatedly, at certain times of the day or night, but seems to want nothing? Is your formerly fastidious feline now using the bathmat or rocker cushion as a substitute litter pan?

If you've had your cat checked out physically, and he has received a clean bill of health, chances are he has lapsed into senility. To be more specific, he may be suffering from cognitive dysfunction

Stepping Outside the Box

Litter box avoidance is one of the two most common causes of "breakups" between cats and their owners (the other is clawing furniture). If your cat has suddenly begun to use other, inappropriate places as his toilet, don't get mad, get logical. Once you've ruled out the obvious (you're keeping the pan clean, have confirmed there is no underlying physical cause, etc.), you may find the answer is right under your nose. Many cats are very picky about the kind of litter they prefer. Perhaps you changed brands, and your cat doesn't like the new one (for example, a number don't like the scented type—the smell is for you, not them). Or maybe it's time to think about changing brands (some older cats, whose paws and claws have become more sensitive, can no longer tolerate the chunkier clay litters).

syndrome (CDS). Only a thorough workup by your vet can determine this, but you'll want to find out as soon as possible because, as in humans, there is no cure, but proper diet and exercise are believed to slow down the progression of this disease, and new medications that offer hope are becoming available.

Signs: meowing/howling, loudly, for no apparent reason; sleeplessness; pacing; confusion/disorientation; failure to recognize family; uncharacteristic aggressiveness and/or anxiety; change in litter box habits
Associated diseases/disorders/conditions: senility, cognitive dysfunction syndrome (CDS); hearing and/or vision impairment or loss

SUMMARY

If it seems there's a lot to absorb in this chapter, keep in mind you don't have to remember all the details, just the concept of awareness, of tuning into the signals your cat may be sending you. In the future, you'll be surprised how much you recall when, say, your cat has a bout of diarrhea, suddenly loses his appetite, or develops an insatiable thirst. You may not remember what those signs mean exactly, but you will know you need to address them. And that's everything. Well, not quite, but it's a great start to everything you can do to take proper care of your aging cat.

KEY PET POINTS

- Keep track of signals from your cat that he is undergoing age-related changes. (Use the checklist in Chapter 2 as a starting point, and add to it as necessary so that you can present it to your vet at your cat's next checkup.)
- Never assume any changes you notice are just "due to getting old," and ignore them.
- Inform yourself about the problems that may be associated with your cat's physical and behavioral changes, but never self-diagnose based on this information.

PART 2

Geriatric Feline Health Care

CHAPTER 4

Wellness Programs: Keeping Your Cat Healthy for the Long Term

Traditionally, health care was for the sick. Doctors were consulted only when something was wrong. Later, the concept of preventive medicine emerged, with the realization that many illnesses and diseases could be forestalled or more effectively managed by taking proper precautions. Preventive measures were also seen as a way to reduce health care costs, for clients, practitioners, and insurance companies alike. But the focus was still on sickness and disease. Today, the approach to health care is distinctly positive: the focus is on *wellness*, and maintaining it for as long as possible.

A skeptic, of course, might regard the term "wellness program" as just the latest in health care jargon, rather than as a legitimate method to improve the way health care is practiced. But even if using the word "wellness" serves the purpose of changing our attitude, might it not be valuable for that reason alone? Isn't it better to think "healthy" instead of "sick," and direct our attention to staying well for as long as possible?

That's certainly the objective of veterinary wellness programs, which are now almost universally being implemented in veterinary practices and hospitals across the country. Gone are the days when vets expected to see pets only in emergencies and for such things as law-mandated vaccinations or flea and tick control. Today, vets recommend that all pets receive an annual checkup and, beginning at age seven, biannual—twice yearly—exams.

Cat-egorically Common

Among geriatric cats, the most common health problems are:

- Diabetes mellitus
- Hyperthyroidism
- Cancer
- Cardiomyopathy (heart disease)
- Kidney disease (chronic renal failure, CRF)
- Dietary issues (obesity or special needs)
- Periodontal disease (dental disease)
- Hypertension (high blood pressure)
- Inflammatory bowel disease
- Skin tumors

In no category of pet care is the concept of wellness more important than the geriatric age group. Says Dr. Richard Goldston: "It has been repeatedly documented that many of the chronic disorders and disease processes seen in geriatric pets can be either cured or at least medically controlled if they are detected early enough." That's why this chapter is devoted in large part to explaining what's involved in standard wellness exams, which can be broadly divided into two categories:

- Exams for healthy-appearing cats
- Exams for sick or unhealthy cats

National Pet Wellness Month: Helping Vets Help Pets

In 2004, the American Veterinary Medical Association (AVMA) teamed with Fort Dodge Animal Health, a division of the Wyeth pharmaceutical company and manufacturer and distributor of animal health care products, to launch National Pet Wellness Month (NPWM), a two-pronged year-round initiative designed to: (1) educate pet owners about the importance of biannual wellness exams, and (2) aid veterinarians in implementing wellness programs into their practices and improving practitioner–pet owner communications.

The level of support in the veterinary community was evident in the turnout for the inaugural campaign, held in October 2004: more than ten thousand veterinary clinics, comprising some 40 percent of all clinics in the United States, signed up.

For more on this campaign and consumer information on veterinary wellness programs, visit either www.npwm.com or www.avma.org.

But before you can take your cat for her wellness exam, you must have a veterinarian. Ideally, you already have one—someone who has been working with you and your cat since your first days together, and is very familiar with your cat's history and health status. If you do, you can skip the next section for now, referring to it later if you need to (for example, if you need a second opinion at some point down the road). But if you do not already have a vet, don't wait to begin your search for one. This must be the first step in any senior cat wellness program.

FINDING A VET

What's the best way to find a vet who interacts well with you and your cat and provides quality care? First, you need to identify the criteria you'll use to find the right vet, which may include:

Starting Now

It's never too late to begin a wellness program for your cat. Even if you've been lucky—your cat has had no health problems so far—so you haven't been taking her to see a vet regularly, now is the best time to start, for both of you. Beginning a regular care program now, no matter how old your cat, will pay off in the future, either by preventing costly problems later or making it possible to manage health care concerns more effectively.

- Location
- Hours of service
- Range of services. For example, can surgery be performed at the office, or would you have to take your cat to another location?
- Type of practice. Is it traditional, holistic, or integrative (combines traditional with holistic/alternative)?
- Hospital and professional affiliations. Is the doctor a member of the AVMA, for example?
- Emergency care handling. Is there a twenty-four-hour on-call service?
- Fee/payment structure
- Personal approach. Do you feel comfortable with the behavior of the vet, technicians, and office staff?
- Ability to communicate. Does the vet explain things clearly and in lay terms, so that you can understand your pet's condition and what's expected of you? Will the vet or someone on staff be available to train you if you need help medicating or treating your cat—from giving a pill (which is never as easy at home as it looks in the vet's office) to administering injections to a cat with diabetes?

After you've identified your criteria, you might want to take the additional step of prioritizing them. For example, if you're on a tight

Who's Who in Pet Health Care: American Veterinary Medical Association (AVMA)

The AVMA, a not-for-profit organization founded in 1863, represents more than seventy-two thousand veterinarians working in private and corporate sectors, government, industry, academia, and uniformed services. Its stated mission is to "improve animal and human health and to advance the veterinary medical profession." The AVMA Web site, www.avma.org, is primarily for its members, but public information is available from its "Animal Health" and "News" links.

budget, fee/payment structure may take precedence over location. Or, to you, the most important criterion may be to work with someone who is willing to consider alternative treatment options before, or in conjunction with, prescription medications. Obviously, your choices could be limited, or virtually unlimited, depending on where you live. Big-city dwellers can pick and choose among numerous vets, whereas rural dwellers may have access to only one practice within a twenty-five-mile (or more) radius.

Generally, pet owners find their veterinarians in one of three ways:

Recommendation. This is far and away the preferred way to go. Ask a friend, family member, or other cat owner (cat lovers have a bond, even when they don't know each other well). Just remember, though, a vet that's right for one person and cat may not be right for you and yours. As in all things involved in your pet's care, trust your instincts and do your homework.

Vet-to-Pet Service

Doctors making house calls to human patients has long been a thing of the past. Our pets are more fortunate. In many areas of the country, you can get vet-to-pet service, which you may want to consider for a number of reasons:

- Perhaps your pet panics in the vet's office (a very common trauma). In her own home, where she is more secure, more "herself," the vet can more easily and accurately evaluate her condition—especially her behavior.
- If your cat is very old and has a compromised immune system for any reason, you reduce the risk of her being exposed to the infections of other sick animals by having her examined at home.
- Your cat may be at the end of her life and you're providing hospice care, with the help of your vet (more on this in Chapter 9).
- You have more than one animal, and rather than having to take them in one at a time, the house-call vet can do a group exam where it's convenient for you.
- Maybe you have no transportation, or you, yourself, are incapacitated for some reason but your pet needs care.

If you're lucky, your vet may provide this service; or if your vet does not generally provide this service, he or she may in special circumstances, such as for a very old or sick cat. If not, and you need to find a vet who makes house calls in your area, contact the American Association of Housecall Veterinarians (AAHV) at www.athomevet.org.

Breed clubs. If yours is a purebred cat, these organizations may be the place to go for referrals to qualified vets. When it comes to cat breeds, it seems there's a club for every one. Or go to the Cat Fanciers' Association Web site, www.cfainc.org, which lists as its first objective "the promotion of the welfare of cats and the improvement of their breed."

Veterinary directories. Whether online or through the Yellow Pages, if you choose this option, it's a good idea to choose at least three names and "vet" them all.

Once you have the name of a vet, schedule an appointment to meet with him or her. You might want to consider going cat-less to this first meeting, so that you can really focus on how the office is run, evaluate whether it's clean and orderly (give it the sniff test, too), and watch how other animals and their owners are treated. Ask for a tour of the facilities (keeping in mind that some rooms may be off-limits due to ongoing treatment or surgery). No conscientious vet will refuse this request; if he or she does, keep looking. Ask for a copy of the practice's policies and procedures. (Note: Expect to pay for "vetting the vet," too.)

If the vet passes the people test, schedule an appointment for your cat's first checkup, and base your final decision on how that is conducted.

I Swear . . .

In November 1999, the American Veterinary Medical Association (AVMA) adopted the following practitioner's oath:

> Being admitted to the profession of veterinary medicine, I solemnly swear to use my scientific knowledge and skills for the benefit of society through the protection of animal health, the relief of animal suffering, the conservation of animal resources, the promotion of public health, and the advancement of medical knowledge.
>
> I will practice my profession conscientiously, with dignity, and in keeping with the principles of veterinary medical ethics.
>
> I accept as a lifelong obligation the continual improvement of my professional knowledge and competence.

Who Ya Gonna Call?

Pet owners turn most often to veterinarians for information about their pets (78 percent according to the Purina's State of the American Pet Survey, and 98 percent according to the AAHA's 2004 Pet Owner Survey). But more frequently today, many are also doing preliminary and/or supplementary research online, especially to obtain more specific information on diseases or drugs.

One final important point here: Though the caseload of many—maybe most—veterinarians in this country today is made up of a high percentage of senior and geriatric animals, that does not mean that all vets are equally capable of handling the numerous problems presented by this population. If, for whatever reason, you feel that your cat is not getting the proper care (again, trust your instincts), waste no time in seeking a second opinion, consulting a veterinary specialist, or finding a new primary caregiver who is better equipped to give her—and you—the care you both need and deserve.

Sunshine: An ear of distinction

THE STORY OF SUNSHINE: THE HEART OF THE MATTER

Sunshine was found in a grocery store. A flyer on the bulletin board just inside the entryway to the market attracted the attention of a woman whose only intent that day was to shop for the family's groceries. "Free Siamese Kittens," it read, above a picture of three blue-eyed youngsters.

Her young daughter, Gail, had been mourning the loss of the family cat, but had been forbidden by her father to "bring another cat into this house" (three dogs already crowded the small home). But some things are meant to be, and Gail's mother "just had a feeling." That evening, after calling the phone number on the flyer and learning there was only a female kitten left (which was the one Gail wanted), mother and daughter set off to find the house. "Love at first sight" barely describes the instant attachment that took place between this heartsick young girl and the kitten who was the cure. The owners handed Gail the kitten, who promptly climbed on her right shoulder and snuggled under her ear. That was that.

Showing no fear of leaving the only family she had ever known, nor of the first car she had ever been in, like a guardian angel she sat on Gail's shoulder all the way to her new home. They were from the start, and remained, inseparable.

The kitten's self-assurance never wavered that first night, not even in the face of three boisterous, tail-thumping, curious dogs, each many times larger than the eight-week-old kitten. She sat on Gail's lap in the rocking chair, like a queen greeting her subjects. And when one of the dogs got too nosey, she gave the sniffer a swat, wasting no time in establishing boundaries of her own design. Soon, though, the kitten and the dogs became the best of friends, playing tag and hide-and-seek until they were all exhausted. Then the kitten could be found curled up with one of them, sleeping it off.

Gail named the kitten Sunshine, after a popular song of the time, "Sunshine on My Shoulders," for that continued to be the cat's favorite perch, even after she was fully grown and had difficulty balancing across Gail's shoulders. When she wasn't on Gail, she was not far away. Another favorite place was across Gail's schoolbooks and papers. Everyone joked that Sunshine was getting an education, too.

Sunshine, thankfully, was mostly a very healthy kitten, for the family did not have a budget that could accommodate frequent veterinary care. She did suffer repeated urinary tract infections until she was spayed, and thereafter was trouble-free until she and Gail had both graduated from college. Then she had a number of bothersome ear infections in her left ear flap, which eventually required minor surgery, leaving her with one wrinkled ear. Gail liked to think of it as Sunshine's "ear of distinction."

But bigger trouble was brewing, though it remained sight unseen for a number of years. At the time, Gail was unaware of the importance of biannual checkups for older cats or of the necessity of feeding quality cat food, and so Sunshine rarely was taken to the veterinarian and was raised on grocery-store cat food (she loved the kind in pouches). Over time, she became a little "chunky." And because they were so attached, Gail took Sunshine everywhere with her, including yearly trips to visit her favorite aunt in Chicago. Often, the cat had to travel in the unpressurized baggage area, which can be stressful to an animal's heart and lungs. Back and forth they went, year after year, until they finally moved permanently to the Big City.

One Sunday night, while Gail was setting out her clothes for work the next day, she suddenly heard an ear-splitting, gut-wrenching sound—Sunshine was yowling. She ran to find the cat stretched across the threshold to the bathroom, panting and breathing heavily. Frantic, Gail started calling vets' offices from the phone directory (she knew hardly anyone in the city and didn't have a vet). It took a number of calls to find one with weekend emergency services. Then, in a cab, they sped across town, where Gail was told Sunshine had had a heart attack and a stroke, the vet guessed, within seconds of each other. For four days they were separated, while Sunshine remained at the clinic for treatment. On the fifth day, when Gail went to pick her up, she was amazed to find the cat strolling around the vet's office as if she owned the place. As she had done wherever she had gone all her life, Sunshine had charmed everyone.

Armed with pills and instructions, home they went. And for two weeks, Sunshine acted like nothing had ever been wrong. But then one night, she just didn't seem quite "there" anymore. Wherever she lay, she would turn to face the wall; and sometimes could be found with her head hanging over the water bowl, not drinking. Gail vowed to take her back to the vet first thing the next morning.

But when she woke to find Sunshine not in bed with her (where she always was), she knew immediately that her worst fears had come true: Sunshine's heart had stopped beating sometime in the night.

THE WELLNESS EXAM

Whether your senior cat appears healthy, is experiencing signs of illness, or has a preexisting disease or disorder, the standard wellness exam will have these elements:

- History
- Complete physical exam
- Screening tests
- Diet and exercise considerations
- Behavior evaluation
- Pharmacological considerations
- Immunizations (vaccinations)

The exact composition of tests and considerations will, however, be based on your cat's age and health status at the time of the exam.

Share the Wellness

It's official: pets are good for our health. So say the scientists who study such things, and in increasing numbers.

As if we didn't already know. Anyone who has felt the stress of a difficult day melt away as their cat lies curled and purring in their lap knows that the best medicine comes not in capsule form, but in fur form. But in no demographic are the pet-to-people benefits so dramatic as among senior citizens.

THE FACTS

Consider these priceless advantages to seniors living with a pet, as reported by the Pet Food Institute:

- A study of Medicare recipients reported that seniors sharing their lives with pets had 21 percent fewer visits to the doctor.
- A study of heart patients revealed that people who owned pets had lower blood pressure and cholesterol levels.
- Seniors with pets report fewer incidences of depression and are less lonely.

That's not all: seniors with pets exercise more; they are more active socially; and in the process of taking care of their pets, they take better care of themselves.

According to the *International Journal of Aging and Human Development*, many Americans would rather live in a place that allows pets than in a more convenient place that doesn't. Fortunately, today all states now allow pets in nursing homes. (Did you know it's against the law for federally assisted senior facilities to discriminate against pet owners? Pass it on.) And the *Journal of the American Geriatrics Society* reported, in May 1999, that seniors living alone with pets tend to have better physical health and a sense of well-being than those without a furry friend.

Even those senior citizens who don't have their own pets can benefit by visits from them. Hospitals and nursing homes that support "pet therapy" programs report patients are more receptive to treatment, have greater incentive to recover, and a stronger will to live.

SENIOR-PET MATCHUP PROGRAMS

In recognition of the good that pets can do for senior citizens, and vice versa, a number of programs have been developed to encourage these relationships. Here are two:

- *Pets for the Elderly Foundation (PEF).* This nonprofit organization "provides the gift of health and happiness to senior citizens in need" by making donations to animal shelters across America for the purpose of providing the elderly with a companion pet at no charge (including adoption fee, spay/neuter fee, immunizations, and follow-up visits). Approximately fifty-five shelters nationwide participate in the program, which has saved nearly five thousand pets—and, of course, brought joy into the lives of many seniors. For more on the PEF, go to www.petsfortheelderly.org; or call 866-849-3598, toll-free.
- *Partnering Animals with Seniors (P.A.W.S.).* Launched by the Arizona Humane Society (AHS), P.A.W.S. is for people sixty or older who want to share their lives with a pet. According to AHS Online, the focus of P.A.W.S. is to find homes for older companion animals in its care—a classic senior matchup. For more on P.A.W.S., go to www.azhumane.org.

To find out if such a program exists in your community, contact your local humane organization, the headquarters of the Humane Society of the United States (HSUS) [202-452-1100; www.hsus.org], or the American Society for the Prevention of Cruelty to Animals (ASPCA) [212-876-7700; www.aspca.org].

Coming to Terms

You may have noticed the terms "healthy-appearing" and "apparently healthy" used in this chapter. It's not hedging. Vets use these phrases for clarity and precision. Recall that your cat may seem perfectly healthy to you, but in fact have "subclinical" indications of a problem, meaning that your cat is showing no signs that she can feel or that you can see.

History

The first stage of the wellness exam is, essentially, a background check—your cat's history. If this is your cat's first visit, expect it to be more comprehensive than if you have a prior relationship with the vet and he or she already has your cat's *baseline data*—the initial set of observations to use for future comparison.

To compile a comprehensive history on your cat's health, your vet will probably ask you both yes/no-type questions and more open-ended questions in a number of categories. He or she may also ask you to fill out a printed historical record, similar to those you fill out prior to your own physical exam. So come prepared to answer questions covering these topics:

- Medications (including prescription, over-the-counter, vitamins, and herbs)
- Previous surgeries or other procedures
- Behavioral changes (See the sidebar "Deadly Behavior" to understand the importance of this topic to your cat's health care.)
- Physical changes
- Appetite
- Level of activity/exercise
- Quality of life

Questions in these categories will apply whether your cat appears healthy, is showing signs of disease/dysfunction, or has already been diagnosed with one or more diseases/disorders. However, if your cat has already been diagnosed, the history questions will be expanded to cover response to/compliance with treatment (therapies, medication, etc.), adherence to/acceptance of dietary changes, and other areas, depending on your cat's specific condition. And if your cat is seriously ill, you'll be asked more in-depth questions about quality of life, so that your vet can better manage pain and other effects of the disease and treatments, as appropriate.

Physical Exam

Your cat's physical exam starts even before the hands-on process begins. The vet does a visual overview—to evaluate posture, quality of gait, signs of stress or discomfort, quality of gaze and coat, and so on. Then the complete physical begins, from "nose to toes," as Dr. Goldston calls it. The *apparently healthy senior cat's* physical will include, but not be limited to, the following, based on her age and history:

Vital signs: temperature, pulse, and respiration (TPR)
Weight: gain or loss, obesity, marked changes in appetite
Musculoskeletal evaluation: mobility, muscle mass, gait, joint "cracking," weakness, and/or pain
Cardiopulmonary evaluation (heart and lungs): heart rate and rhythm, pulse rate and quality, blood pressure
Outer cat: quality of skin, coat, and claws, and nail bed characteristics
Central nervous system: mental activity, nerve reflexes
Eyes and ears: signs of deterioration, infection, or disease
Abdominal: palpation to determine size and shape of kidneys and liver
Mouth: signs of gum or dental disease; quality of care
Other: risk factor analysis; hydration; signs of lymph node enlargement

Taking TPR

Ask your vet what your cat's normal temperature and pulse and heart rate should be. You might also consider learning how to take these vital signs. Knowing how to do this will better enable you to determine when something is wrong at home. Your vet can show you the proper way to take these measurements.

For the *senior cat experiencing signs of disease or disorder*, the physical exam will be more extensive. It will include a detailed evaluation of any organs showing signs of disease or dysfunction. Your cat will also be carefully monitored for indications of cognitive dysfunction syndrome (CDS) such as disorientation, sleep disturbances, confusion, increased anxiety, and change in litter box habits. The diagnosis aspect will focus on these common senior cat problems:

- Arthritis
- Cancers
- Gastrointestinal disorders
- Weight changes
- Cardiac disease
- Renal disease
- Diabetes
- Hyperthyroidism
- Respiratory disorders

The symptoms and changes you have reported to your vet since your last visit, along with the vet's own observations during this checkup, will determine any future testing in these areas (see Chapter 6).

And for the *seriously ill senior cat*, an important focus of the exam will be on pain management, quality of life, and, potentially, hospice

Deadly Behavior

It's not old age, nor age-related disease, that is the reason most pet cats are euthanized in this country. Sadly, the most common reason is because of negative behaviors—the most often cited being destroying furniture and urinating outside the litter box. For that reason, four years ago, the American Association of Feline Practitioners (AAFP) began a study of "what cats did and why." The result was the publication, in 2004, of a forty-two-page report titled "AAFP Feline Behavior Guidelines," compiled by a panel of experts made up of certified behaviorists and feline practitioners. Their objective: to "make behavior assessment a routine part of feline health care."

The guidelines describe normal behaviors in cats from birth through old age and identify behaviors that may indicate either physical or psychological problems. Defining what is normal and abnormal cat behavior was the first step, to enable veterinary practitioners to better educate cat owners, and to be able, themselves, to more accurately identify those behaviors that are signs of underlying medical conditions. The end result, it is hoped, will be "earlier intervention and better clinical outcomes."

Though the guidelines were written for feline veterinary practitioners, most of the information in them is comprehensible to the layperson and well worth a look-see, especially if you are having trouble understanding (or are frustrated by) your cat's behavior. The guidelines are available for download from www.catwellness.org.

And for a more personal approach to your cat's behavior, another good online resource is sponsored by PBS, the Public Broadcasting System. Go to www.pbs.org/wgbh/nova/vets, and click on "Don't Blame Your Pet," "Ask the Behaviorists," and/or "Resources."

Who's Who in Pet Health Care: The American Association of Feline Practitioners (AAFP)

The AAFP is a professional veterinary organization that "seeks to raise the standards of feline medicine and surgery among practitioners." To that end, it sponsors continuing education programs, rewards advances in research, and supports the American Board of Veterinary Practitioners (ABVP) certification in the Feline Practice category. For more information about this organization, visit www.aafponline.org.

care, all of which you'll learn more about later in the book. Behavior problems will be major considerations, too, as these become more apparent with increased loss of mobility and increased pain or anxiety.

Screening Tests

For cat owners, this is often the most challenging aspect of the wellness exam because most of it takes place out of their sight. For example, although you probably will be present when your cat's blood is drawn, the actual screening of the blood will be done in a lab by a technician doing procedures you wouldn't understand even if you could be present. What's more, the language of medical testing is unintelligible to most pet owners, unless they happen to work in the medical profession, too.

That said, it's still a good idea to familiarize yourself with the common screening tests your cat will undergo as part of her wellness exam. For a *healthy-appearing senior cat*, these include:

- Complete blood count
- Complete urinalysis
- Blood pressure
- Internal parasite exam (for heartworm and internal parasites)
- Fecal analysis
- Serum creatinine (test of kidney function, run in conjunction with urinalysis)
- Total bilirubin (test for jaundice, which may indicate a liver problem)
- Total protein levels (test for disorders of the intestines, kidneys, liver, decreased nutrient intake, and more)
- Total calcium levels (elevated levels are a sign of a number of diseases, including lymphosarcoma, a very common cancer among cats)
- Blood sugar (glucose; as increased levels may be a sign of diabetes)
- Additional tests, as necessary based on age, breed, sex, medical history, and current medications (e.g., feline leukemia virus (FeLV) antigen test and feline immunodeficiency virus (FIV) antibody test, if not done previously or if your cat is at risk)

For the *senior cat experiencing signs of disease or disorder*, expect the screening tests to include those listed above, plus:

- Confirmatory tests
- Biopsies, if necessary
- As required: X-rays, ultrasound, echocardiography, and contrast studies
- Others, based on condition

Nutrition and Exercise

The findings of the physical exam and the screening tests will enable your vet to develop a nutritional plan that's right for your aging cat. According to Dr. Goldston:

Many new diets have been precisely formulated for older pets having high-risk factors for certain diseases, or for those

Learn Your ABCs

If you've ever watched hospital shows on television, you've no doubt been stupefied by the shorthand doctors use to refer to various tests and procedures. Vets are no different. To help you navigate the alphabet soup, here are some of the most common abbreviations you may hear in the vet's office or see on invoices or other paperwork regarding your cat:

- BCP: blood chemistry profiles
- CBC: complete blood count
- CRF: chronic renal failure
- FCV: feline calicivirus (infection of dental oral cavity and respiratory system)
- FeLV: feline leukemia virus
- FIV: feline immunodeficiency virus (causes feline AIDS)
- FIP: feline infectious peritonitis
- FVR: feline viral rhinotracheitis (most common upper respiratory infection in cats)
- IBD: inflammatory bowel disease
- UA: urinalysis

Any others you hear or see and don't understand, ask!

having early degenerative aging changes in various organ systems. Choosing and feeding a diet scientifically formulated for a specific organ disorder, such as kidney failure, heart disease, liver or pancreatic insufficiency, digestive disorders, and so on, will slow down the degenerative processes and either improve the organ function or, in some cases, reduce the workload of the organ. This will improve how your pet feels and may prolong its life. It's a win-win situation for you and your pet.

Based on the results of those two wellness exam components, your vet may recommend, for example:

- Increasing your cat's protein intake (*unless* your cat has been diagnosed with renal disease).
- Switching to one of the stage-of-life diets—for example, premium "senior" or "less active" brands, if you buy her food from a grocery store or pet supply store; or to a "prescription" cat food, which is available for purchase only from veterinary offices.
- Adding an antioxidant to your cat's diet.
- Starting an exercise program.

And if your cat is overweight or obese, your vet no doubt will recommend a weight reduction program; or in the case of a diagnosed disease, a therapeutic diet to help manage it. Finally, you'll be asked to begin to carefully monitor your cat's consumption of both water and food.

These two components of your cat's health program are covered more fully in the next chapter, "Keeping Your Cat in Shape: Nutrition, Exercise, and Grooming."

Medications, Herbs, and Supplements

As with nutrition and diet, this segment of the exam is entirely dependent on the findings of the complete physical and screening tests. And any remedies chosen will depend in part on whether you take your cat to a veterinarian who practices traditional, holistic, or integrative medicine, or if you work with more than one type of practitioner. Chapter 6 will give you more information on these topics.

Vaccinations

You won't find anyone in the veterinary medical community who will dispute the value of vaccinations (immunizations, "shots") to pets and the pet-owning public. These vaccines have saved the lives

Lurking in the Shadows

Vaccines work by triggering protective immune responses. Some can reduce the severity of future diseases, while others can prevent infection altogether. Thanks to vaccines, from time to time throughout history, certain widespread infectious diseases became so uncommon that they were believed to have been eradicated and that vaccinations were longer necessary. In fact, the disease agents continue to be present in the environment, lying in wait for the right opportunity and host to reemerge, as deadly as ever. So vaccines continue to be an essential element in preventive health care. But more is being learned every day about how, and how often, vaccines should be administered in any population, whether human or animal.

---

of millions of animals; and in the case of cats specifically, they have halted widespread deaths caused by panleukopenia (feline distemper), upper respiratory infections, feline leukemia, rabies, and many others. Thus, for years, vaccinations were given routinely every year. More recently, however, it has been discovered that

some vaccines provide immunity that lasts much longer than a year, and that others offer protection for less than a year. Moreover, it has been found that some cats that get yearly shots are at risk of developing tumors, called *sarcomas*, at the immunization site.

Both these issues raise the question of the wisdom of vaccinating an older cat—particularly a much older cat. That is why, today, standard practice is to design customized vaccination programs for each pet, taking into consideration factors such as age, health, and environment (certain diseases are more prevalent in certain parts of the country than others).

Lifestyle, too, is taken into account. If your cat rarely goes out and comes into contact with other cats only infrequently, she is probably at less risk of exposure to infectious disease. Local laws also are part of the equation. Most counties and many states have rabies vaccination laws that mandate how often your pet must be vaccinated.

To help customize your cat's vaccination program, your vet should consider, at a minimum, these factors:

- Your cat's age and current health status
- Your cat's current and future risk of exposure (e.g., you plan to go away in the near future and board your cat)
- Protective capability of the vaccine
- Reactions your cat has had to previous immunizations

As a pet owner, it's wise to take a proactive stance when it comes to vaccinations. Whenever your vet recommends immunizing your cat, ask what the vaccine is for exactly and why your cat needs it.

Cat-chy: Infectious Diseases in Cats

The following list (in alphabetical order) identifies a number of the infectious diseases your cat may be exposed to in her lifetime, and for which immunizations exist. As stated previously, which of these protections your cat needs must be evaluated on an individual basis.

- *Feline Calcivirus (FCV).* A major upper respiratory virus that is highly contagious and widespread. Signs include fever, pneumonia, and sores or blisters on the tongue.

- *Feline Chlamydiosis.* Another feline respiratory disease that is extremely contagious, especially in young kittens. This one, caused by the *Chlamydia psittaci* bacterium, has symptoms that include conjunctivitis, sneezing, salivation, and coughing.
- *Feline Infectious Peritonitis (FIP).* This viral disease is most common in young adult cats. Once symptoms become apparent, FIP becomes progressive and leads to death. Though risk of FIP is lower than other infectious diseases, there is no cure and diagnosis testing is difficult.
- *Feline Leukemia Virus (FeLV).* This virus, transmitted by cat-to-cat contact—hence, it is most common in multicat environments such as shelters, catteries, and multicat households—is a leading cause of death in cats. The virus is dangerous in two ways: the leukemia itself can cause death, and it breaks down a cat's immune system, so that she can no longer fight off other infections.
- *Feline Panleukopenia (Feline Distemper).* This highly contagious viral disease typically affects young kittens (with a high mortality rate), but all cats, depending on circumstance, may be susceptible. Loss of appetite, vomiting, diarrhea, and dehydration are common symptoms.
- *Feline Viral Rhinotracheitis (FVR).* This, the most dangerous upper respiratory virus that affects cats, is highly contagious, with symptoms ranging from fever, eye and nose discharge, coughing, and mouth breathing. FVR attacks cats of all ages, though kittens are more prone to it.
- *Rabies.* The most well-known of infectious diseases affecting all mammals (including humans) is transmitted by contact with the saliva of an infected animal. Outdoor cats are at high risk, though indoor cats with even occasional outdoor access may be exposed. In most areas of the country, rabies vaccination is required by law.
- *Ringworm.* This is a fungal infection typified by dry, flaky skin and hair loss. Seen most commonly in multicat environments, it's important to note that ringworm can also infect humans.

THE YOU FACTOR

There's one other component of the wellness exam, and it has everything to do with you: it's the point during the exam when your veterinarian educates you—whether it's to emphasize the importance of brushing your cat's teeth, to inform you about the signs of change to watch for in your cat between this visit and the next, or to advise you how to keep your old cat mentally stimulated if she's beginning to show the signs of senility. At a minimum, look for your vet to review with you:

- The common diseases/syndromes of older cats and your role in helping to detect them
- The importance of compliance in giving medications exactly as prescribed
- The importance of controlling weight—monitoring either for gain or loss—and sticking to an exercise regimen (including mental stimulation)

Campaigning for Cats

In conjunction with its "Feline Behavior Guidelines" described earlier in the chapter, the American Association of Feline Practitioners (AAFP), in cooperation with Fort Dodge Animal Health (a division of Wyeth pharmaceuticals), sponsored "The Great Cat Watch, for Wellness Sake" campaign to educate cat owners on how to recognize the subtle signs of sickness in their cats. The campaign Web site (www.catwellness.org) has a wealth of easy-to-access and easy-to-understand information. Go to the Cats Corner at the bottom of the home page, for example, and click on one of three info-packed links: "Feeding Your Cat (Preventing Obesity)," "The Litter Pan Alley," and "Behavioral Problems." You can also view a video from the site that explains why cats hide their illness.

- The significance of keeping a log of your cat's progress and changes
- Environmental adjustments you may need to make to accommodate disability or weakness and to maintain quality of life
- If necessary, the benefit of spaying/neutering

SUMMARY

Legendary actress Bette Davis said, "Getting old is not for sissies." She was right, of course. Caring for an aging loved one is not for sissies, either. But when you take your cat for biannual wellness exams, you give yourself a leg up on the process: you know where she stands, healthwise; you partner with your vet, so you know you have support at all times; and you prepare yourself for your responsibilities. The reward, of course, is more and better-quality time with your favorite feline.

It won't be easy a lot of the time. And in the next chapter, we take on three aspects of senior cat care that many pet owners find the most challenging: nutrition, exercise, and grooming.

KEY PET POINTS

- The best start to giving your aging cat the care she needs is to put yourself in a "wellness" mind-set.
- Interview your vet as you would any professional person providing you with a service. Take into account both your needs and the needs of your aging cat. Do not hesitate to seek second opinions, consult with veterinary specialists, or switch to a new primary vet.
- Prepare yourself for the extensive nature of the standard geriatric wellness exam. Whether your cat appears healthy or already has some age-related health issues, she will receive a comprehensive physical exam and standard tests, plus other evaluations depending on her age and condition.
- Clarify what you will be required to do in carrying out the recommendations of your cat's vet following the wellness exam.

Geriatric Pet Examination Summary

At the conclusion of your geriatric pet's examination, your vet may provide you with a summary similar to this one, including recommendations for future medical care.

Date: _____

	Appears Normal	Medical Attention Required
Skin and coat condition	__________	______________
Teeth and mouth	__________	______________
Legs and paws	__________	______________
Heart and lungs	__________	______________
Gastrointestinal/fecal exam	__________	______________
Urinary and genital/urinalysis	__________	______________
Eyes, ears, nose, and throat	__________	______________
Brain and spine	__________	______________
Diet/nutrition/weight	__________	______________
Parasite control		
Blood chemistry profile/CBC	__________	______________
Chest X-rays and cardiac exam	__________	______________
Other	__________	______________

Vaccinations: Up to date ______ Recommended ______________

Recommendations/medical attention needed:

____

____

____

____

____

____

____

____

Source: Reprinted with permission of VCA St. Petersburg Animal Hospital, St. Petersburg, Florida.

CHAPTER 5

Keeping Your Cat in Shape: Nutrition, Exercise, and Grooming

Nearly every day it seems, we hear or read something about the importance of proper nutrition and adequate exercise to maintaining our health. It's no different for our cats. So you will already be familiar with many of the concepts presented in this chapter. That's the good news. The bad news is, many pet owners have as much difficulty implementing effective diet and exercise programs for their pets as they do for themselves. Therefore, in addition to explaining the specific effects of diet and exercise on aging cats, a primary objective here is to convince you of the importance of incorporating regimens for both in your cat's health care program.

The significance of the third topic of this chapter—grooming—may also take some convincing, for it's not something every cat owner thinks about, because, as everyone knows, cats groom themselves. It's even one of their "selling" features for people who are considering the kind of pet they want; some people think of it as a convenience of sorts. But, in fact, it's essential to augment your cat's natural grooming behavior—whether he is young or old—for a number of reasons beneficial to both you and your cat:

- Lowers the incidence of hairballs
- Reduces shedding
- Acts as a bonding ritual for you and your cat
- Enables you to do a hands-on assessment of your "outer" cat, one of the most effective preventive health measures

For older cats, your helping hands in the grooming department are vitally important, as many geriatric felines become lax in their cleanup routines, some because they've lost flexibility due to a musculoskeletal disorder such as arthritis; others because they're obese and can no longer reach parts of their bodies easily; still others for reasons of senility. But for all, the result is the same: elderly cats that are not groomed properly and on a regular basis are more susceptible to a whole range of problems, which you'll learn about later in the chapter.

THE PATH TO GOOD NUTRITION

Ideally, you have already taken the first step on the path to good nutrition for your senior cat, by taking him for his first of two wellness exams this year. At that time, your vet should have given you what Dr. Goldston calls a "nutritional consultation" based on the findings of the physical exam and the screening tests he or she conducted. (If your vet did not, ask for it.)

As the metabolism of older cats slows, usually it becomes necessary to reduce their caloric intake accordingly. Even if your cat weighs the same as he did during his more active years, his muscle-to-fat ratio has changed. Though your cat may have maintained a steady weight of, say, ten pounds since his young-adult years, the content of those pounds will have changed: the percentage of fat weight increases while the percentage of lean muscle weight decreases.

Obesity: It's Not Just for People Anymore

One in four cats and dogs in the western world is overweight or obese, according to the National Academies: Advisors to the Nation on Science, Engineering and Medicine, making obesity the most common nutritional problem in pets today. Though still lagging behind the 50 percent of the human population estimated to be obese, cats are catching up, with an accompanying rise in associated health problems—among them diabetes, heart problems, arthritis, and a shortened lifespan. Aggravating the risk is that excess weight makes it more difficult for veterinarians to do their job. Dr. Goldston says the most common cause of disease/ailment in aging pets that we *can control* is overfeeding.

Top factors contributing to obesity are: age, spay/neuter status, type of diet, "free" and treat feeding, portion size, and level of exercise. The first factor, obviously, you can do nothing about; the benefits of the second, spaying/neutering your cat, outweigh its implication in weight gain. But the others you *can* do something about. If your cat is overweight or obese, ask yourself:

- Have you switched to a reduction diet food, as recommended by your vet?
- How much and how often are you feeding your cat? Do you use a measuring cup or just pour food into the bowl?
- Do you "free feed" dry food—filling the bowl so your pet can eat whenever he wants?
- How many treats do you give your cat every day? What kind?
- Do you give in when your cat begs for table or kitchen scraps?
- Does more than one person in your household feed your cat?
- Does your cat have access to another pet's food?
- Do you exercise your cat regularly?

Your answers may give you some clues as to why and how your cat packed on the pounds. Work with your vet on a diet program for your cat and monitor your cat's weight closely. His life depends on it.

Your vet may have suggested a feeding protocol, or schedule, along with instructions to include *nutraceuticals* in your cat's diet. These are fortified foods or dietary supplements that provide health benefits in addition to their basic nutritional value. A feeding schedule or protocol based on your cat's individual condition might include:

- Reduction in number of calories consumed each day
- A ban on free feeding, the practice of keeping your cat's bowl or feeder filled at all times so that he can eat whenever he feels like it. Easy for you, but this can lead to obesity, especially if yours is an indoor cat, left alone for much of the day with

Who's Who in Pet Health Care: Cornell University College of Veterinary Medicine Feline Health Center

Cornell University's Feline Health Center (FHC) is a veterinary medical specialty center with a two-pronged objective: (1) to conduct and sponsor feline health studies for the purpose of learning new ways to prevent and cure cat diseases; and (2) to educate both veterinary practitioners and cat owners by providing up-to-date medical information and to promote awareness and understanding of feline health care issues. As a cat owner, you'll want to become familiar with the offerings of Cornell's informative Web site. Log on to www.vet.cornell.edu, and under Companion Animals, click on either "Feline Health Information" or "CatWatch" (the organization's newsletter, which you can sample and subscribe to); or go directly to the FHC by logging on to www.vet.cornell.edu/FHC; from there, click on "Cat Owner Resources," then "Feline Health Information," to access cat health literature and pet loss support. There's also a link at the Feline Health Center Web site to "Purr-fect Gifts," where you can buy a copy of the most recent edition of the widely acclaimed *The Cornell Book of Cats*, which is an excellent reference for anyone sharing his or her life with an aging cat.

nothing to do but sleep and eat. According to Cornell University's College of Veterinary Medicine Feline Health Center, cats living in apartments are approximately two times more likely to be overweight than cats that live in larger homes or have access to the outdoors, and cats that get no exercise are sixteen times more likely to be obese.

- More feedings but with the same number of daily calories—two or three meals a day instead of one large one, for example—to increase the energy used to digest those calories
- More or less per serving, based on number of feedings

Dangerous Diets

A poor or inappropriate diet may contribute to:

- Obesity, from overfeeding, especially foods high in fat and calories
- Diabetes, from food toxins
- Allergies or food intolerance, from chemical preservatives and poor-quality ingredients
- Heart disease and hypertension, from high-sodium foods
- Some cancers, from chemical preservatives

In terms of supplements, common dietary additions include glucosamine and chondroitin sulfate to relieve joint, muscle, and bone pain; omega fatty acids for dry skin and skin allergies; vitamin E as an antioxidant; vitamin A to boost the immune function and for vision; and minerals such as calcium, potassium, and several others. (See the table "Nutrient Essentials for Cats" for a more complete listing.) But the same precaution applies here as for prescription medications: Never introduce a supplement to your cat's diet without approval from your vet. And be especially careful when you buy cat food, as some of these supplements may already be present in the food, and too much can be just as dangerous as too little. Read the labels!

Nutrient Essentials for Cats

Vitamins	Minerals
Vitamin A	Calcium
Vitamin D	Phosphorus
Vitamin E	Magnesium
Vitamin K	Sodium
Vitamin B1	Potassium
Riboflavin	Chlorine
Vitamin B6	Iron
Niacin	Copper
Pantothenic Acid	Zinc
Vitamin B12	Manganese
Folic Acid	Selenium
	Iodine

Note: For details about the role of each of these vitamins and minerals, as well as signs of too much or too little of them in your cat, go to the National Academies Web site, http://national-academies.org/petdoor.

Who's Who in Pet Health Care: The National Academies: Advisors to the Nation on Science, Engineering and Medicine

In September 2003, in response to the growing problem of pet obesity in the western world, the National Academies released a 450-page report (sponsored by the National Institutes of Health, the Food and Drug Administration, and the Pet Food Institute) described as "the most comprehensive assessment available of the daily nutrient and calorie requirements for dogs and cats." The report was written primarily for a professional audience of veterinarians, pet food manufacturers, and scientists, but the National Academies has made a quick reference available online for the pet-owning public. Go to http://national-academies.org/petdoor to get either dog or cat info. Also be sure to follow the FAQs and the "Did You Know?" links. You'll learn a lot about how to feed your pets and keep them healthy.

If your cat's appetite is not what it used to be—common among older cats—and your vet has confirmed that it is not due to illness or disease or side effects of any medication, he or she may suggest methods to stimulate your cat's flagging interest in food. For example:

- Bring refrigerated food to room temperature before dishing it out, to let the scent of it emerge and entice your cat. Or heat it for a few seconds in the microwave.
- Add beef, chicken, or vegetable broth (no-sodium, of course) or cooked veggies.
- For serious cases, feed by hand.

Everything your vet told you about your cat's nutritional needs will make it much easier to navigate the pet food maze.

Navigating the Food Maze

You know what it's like to stagger down those increasingly long aisles of cat food at the pet superstores, or even your grocery store, wondering how in the world to decide which food to buy your cat. (Commercial pet food is one of the most competitive commodities in the United States.) Perhaps in a moment of weakness you've been swayed by packaging. This is understandable: the $25-billion (worldwide) pet food industry pays its mass-marketers big bucks to learn which colors people prefer, which typefaces and sizes are easiest and most compelling to read, and which container shapes are most appealing to consumers. Because you love your cat and want what's best for him, you want to see past the promotional hoopla and try to interpret what's really in those packages with tempting-sounding text (can a hard-baked dry pellet *really* taste just like fresh tuna or roast chicken?). But it's a forest of adjectives out there—"premium," "superpremium," "low-fat," "high-fiber," "senior," "high-protein," "natural," "organic," and on and on—and a lot of pet owners have trouble finding their way through it.

Let's start with some basics.

Pet Food Overview

There are three primary sources of pet food:

- Commercial brands sold in grocery stores
- Commercial pet foods sold in pet stores and pet food supply houses
- Prescription pet foods available in veterinary offices

Although the commercial selections available in many grocery stores have improved greatly in recent years, most vets agree this source should be your last choice. Understandably, however, many people are tempted to resort to this option for reasons of accessibility and price. Say you've been working late all week, and you're

Going Down the Aisle

While the caution against grocery store–brand cat food remains valid generally, it is only fair to note that more "premium" and "stage-of-life" brand cat foods are being sold in grocery stores today. If one that your vet has approved for your cat is available where you shop, by all means, buy it there. Also note that, according to Dr. Goldston, the higher-quality cat food brands available in grocery stores are always preferable to feeding your cat table foods.

---

cranky and exhausted and just want to go home and relax. But you know your cupboards are bare, so you stop in at a nearby grocery store on your way home and, while pushing your cart in circles, you realize you're out of cat food, too. And there, oh-so-conveniently located in aisle five, is the store's selection of cat food. And it's so much less expensive than the brands at the pet store. Why not?

The answer, Dr. Richard Goldston says, is in the adage "you get what you pay for." Be particularly wary of generic store brands, as compared with brand names, because the quality of the food's protein can vary widely even when the ingredients on the label seem to be identical. How is this possible? You have to consider the source. In the higher-quality food, whose protein source is, let's say, chicken or chicken by-products, the meat is likely to be from the breast and legs, whereas in the cheaper food, it may be from the feet, head, and body-cavity contents. Even protein from grain ingredients may be suspect. For example, it may be from "human-quality" cereal grains such as wheat, soybean, or corn, or from moldy, insect-infested grain deemed unfit for human consumption but approved for use in pet foods. Fat content, too, is a cause for concern. You know by now that there are so-called good fats and bad fats. You're also probably all too familiar with the fact that the "bad" fats, the ones to avoid because they're so difficult to digest and high in calories, often are the very ones that make food taste better. The same is true in pet foods. So if you get your cat used to the bad, but good-tasting fat in cheaper foods, you're going to have a much more difficult time switching him to a better brand later on when he absolutely must have it to help manage an age-related disease or disorder.

If the older pet is healthy, says Dr. Goldston, as many of them are, many good commercial diets are available for them. "The major pet food companies such as Purina, Iams, Eukanuba, Hill's Science Diet, Waltham, and others have a lot of quality products," he says. Here, too, however, you must be careful, as some of these companies also market cheaper foods that may not be adequate for older cats; but their upper-level diets are very good.

For older cats with a specific organ dysfunction such as liver or kidney, or a musculoskeletal problem, Dr. Goldston recommends special prescription diets, which he feels are superior to nonprescription choices. These you'll be able to purchase only through your vet. Hill's Science Diet has the most types and the longest history of producing very high-quality diets for specific organ dys-

Snack Attacks

All this talk about healthy eating may lead you to believe that snacks for your cat are a no-no. And that's true—if you're currently feeding him cat snacks that are the feline equivalent of human junk food, made of grains, flavor enhancers, food coloring, and so on. But if you feed your cat healthy treats, such as small bits of fresh chicken or fish (i.e., natural protein) or a vet-approved commercial snack, you don't have to deprive your cat. One other snack-attack warning: Don't feed your cat a treat as a way to address a behavior problem, such as vocalizing or scratching. When you do this, you're actually supporting the behavior, because your cat will very quickly figure out that he gets rewarded for something you *don't* want him to do.

functions, says Dr. Goldston. These include, for example, i/d (intestinal diet), k/d and u/d (kidney failure diets), u/d and s/d (urinary stone diets), r/d and w/d (weight management diets), and l/d (liver failure diet). He adds, however, that Eukanuba, Waltham, Purina, and others also produce very good prescription diets. He cites the Innovative Veterinary Diets (IVD) company as having the best overall selection for treatment of allergies.

The Joy of Cooking for Cats

A growing trend among pet owners is to prepare homemade cat food. But in considering this option, you must consider carefully the investment in time and effort required. First, there's the learning curve to climb: you must familiarize yourself with what makes up a balanced diet for your cat. To be effective, it will have to contain all the right nutrients, as described earlier. Meeting this requirement becomes more complicated as your cat gets older and develops age-related ailments and disorders. Next, you'll have to shop for all these ingredients—on a regular basis. Then you must prepare the food; and though you can cook in advance to some degree, this will be an ongoing commitment, 365 days a year. So be honest with yourself or you won't be fair to you or your cat. If, for example, you frequently travel on business, is there someone else in your household willing to pick up the spoon and pan in your absence? And if you board your cat when you go away, realize the staff there will not be able to offer home-cooked meals in most cases, meaning your cat will be subjected to a sudden change in diet—never a good idea for cats, especially older ones.

For those willing to make this commitment, however, plenty of help is now available in the form of recipes for cats. And your vet can give you a jumpstart by detailing the components of a balanced diet for your cat, including supplements.

Some words of caution: Don't, in your enthusiasm, begin by throwing out all the store-bought food you have on the shelf.

Again, any diet change must be made gradually. A good plan is to slowly introduce the home-cooked food—two or three times a week, for example. And carefully monitor your cat's appetite and digestion for tolerance: watch for signs of upset, including constipation or diarrhea, gas, vomiting, change in stool, and so on. Bring these changes to the attention of your vet ASAP.

Two books you might want to check out before you make your cat food shopping list are *Dr. Pitcairn's New Complete Guide to Natural Health for Dogs and Cats* by Richard H. Pitcairn, DVM (Rodale Books, 2005); and *Home-Prepared Dog & Cat Diets: The Healthful Alternative* by Donald R. Strombeck (Iowa State University Press, 1999).

In the Raw

A fifth option, feeding your cat raw foods, is somewhat controversial. Proponents contend that cooking and processing destroys important nutrients and that a raw diet most closely resembles how cats eat in the wild, while opponents raise very real safety concerns. Uncooked protein may contain deadly microorganisms—for example, chicken and eggs may contain salmonella. And raw foods must be washed thoroughly and stored properly to prevent contamination. This diet also presents the same challenge to the owner as home cooking: you must ensure a proper balance of minerals, protein, vitamins, and so on, for your cat to be properly nourished.

Information on this trend is widely available online today. One place to start is the incongruously named BARF, which stands for Biologically Appropriate Raw Food, at www.barfworld.com. There's also the more upbeat-named Bravo, offering "foundation food," at www.bravorawdiet.com. But don't make a decision about this diet until you talk it over with your vet. Senior cats' digestive systems tend to be very sensitive, and eating raw just may put them in the rough.

Who's Minding the Store? Regulating Pet Food

You know if you've ever tried to read a label on a can or bag of cat food that it's not easy to do, even with your reading glasses or one of those handy magnifier strips. Often, there's very little on the list that sounds like real food.

Fortunately, for your cat's health—and your peace of mind—there are some organizations and agencies making an effort to monitor and regulate the content of pet food and, in the case of government agencies, establish standards as to what can and cannot be used in it and what can and cannot be said about it on labels and promotional materials. But you won't be surprised to learn that some manufacturers have found ways to get around these standards yet remain within the scope—if not the spirit—of the law.

The details of these efforts are beyond the scope of this book, but the following will give you some background, along with pointers to sources of further information, if you're interested in learning more.

- The U.S. Food and Drug Administration Center for Veterinary Medicine (CVM) regulates the manufacture and distribution of food additives and drugs that will be given to animals. The center is responsible for regulating drugs, devices, and food additives given to, or used on, more than 100 million companion animals (as well as farm animals and other animal species). Go to www.fda.gov/cvm for more on the work of this federal agency.
- The Pet Food Institute (PFI), founded in 1958, calls itself the "voice of U.S. pet food manufacturers," representing the manufacturers of 97 percent of all cat and dog food produced in this country. PFI also serves as the pet food industry's public education and media relations resource and its representative before Congress and federal and state agencies; it also organizes seminars and educational programs. Info on the PFI can be found at www.petfoodinstitute .org.

- The Association of American Feed Control Officials (AAFCO) has as its goal to "provide a mechanism for developing and implementing uniform and equitable laws, regulations, standards, and enforcement policies for regulating the manufacture, distribution, and sale of animal feeds." Certainly sounds like a worthwhile undertaking. Unfortunately, its many detractors in the animal welfare world believe its test protocols are weak, hence the AAFCO "guarantee" on pet food labels is unreliable as a guide to pet owners. For more on AAFCO, go to www.aafco.org.

CHECK, PLEASE

If you've read this far, it should be clear that there's only one easy answer to which diet you should feed your aging or geriatric cat: the one your vet recommends. Beyond that, a few shopping guidelines may help decide what you ultimately put in your shopping cart, and your cat's bowl:

- The most obvious: check the expiration date.
- Look for the AAFCO guarantee: it may not be perfect, but it's a start.
- Look for "named" meats, such as chicken, lamb, or beef—not the generic "meat." Note the grain content: rice is the most digestible; and be on the lookout for more than one mention of corn.
- Beware the word "meal"—either meat or by-product meal—as the first ingredient listed. These rendered products are the cheapest source of protein, and vary widely in terms of quality and content.
- Ignore such claims as "natural," "light," and "healthy." Neither AAFCO nor the FDA regulates these terms. This is marketing jargon, pure and simple, and it can mean whatever the manufacturer wants it to mean.
- Look for natural preservatives, such as vitamins C and E, and avoid the chemical varieties, which include BHA, BHT, ethoxyquin, and

propyl gallate. (If you can't pronounce it, it's probably a chemical additive.)

- Unless your vet has specifically recommended one, avoid any special or stage-of-life formulas, as they may contain ingredients or supplements not appropriate to your cat's condition.
- Again, avoid the generic store brands, which may be manufacturer rejects in new packaging.

Canned or Dry: That Is the Question

There is a good deal of controversy among vets about which is better for cats, canned or dry food. You'll find proponents in both camps who cite the potential problems associated with each type of food. The only thing that should concern you is that your cat is getting the nutrients he needs and in a form that is palatable to him and easy to digest. That is why it is imperative that you monitor your cat's appetite and eating habits and bring any changes to the attention of your vet. The diet he or she recommends should be chosen according to what's right for your cat, based on his age, weight, and physical condition.

And once you get the food home, here are a few other steps you can take to make sure all's well:

1. When you open the bag, box, or can, sniff it. If it smells rancid, close it back up and return it.
2. To be supersafe, transfer dry food to a sealed container; transfer canned food to glass or ceramic containers and refrigerate.
3. To avoid digestion problems, integrate new food into your cat's diet gradually: a ratio of one-third new to two-thirds old is good to start with; then add a little more new food and a little less old food each day.

4. Monitor your cat's acceptance. This includes whether he likes it, how he digests it (watch for vomiting, in particular), and how he eliminates it (check for consistency changes to his stool). Also watch for weight gain or loss and changes to his coat and skin.

One more thing: Don't forget the H_2O. Water is as important a nutrient as any other. Wash out his bowl and put fresh water in it at least once day, and make sure it's filled at all times.

ON THE EXERCISE TRACK

Exercise is so easy to talk about and so very difficult to actually do. We try every trick in the book to get ourselves going, from paying for membership at a gym to signing up for an exercise class to buying expensive space-hogging equipment for our homes. But too often, the membership goes unused, we skip the class, and the equipment becomes just another place to throw our clothes at the end of the day. We know exercise is vital for maintaining our vigor and controlling our weight, yet our follow-through always seems to fall through. So what can be said here to convince you to exercise your older cat, whose primary role in life—admit it now—you've come to see as lap warmer and window decoration? Pet owners seem to have no trouble acknowledging that dogs need regular exercise, but it rarely occurs to them that cats need it, too. Perhaps it's their self-possessed demeanor, the one that seems to say, "You disturbed my nap to have me chase that ball for you? You're kidding, right?"

The answer, for the good of your cat, has to be "right!" Because it is, simply, indisputable that keeping your older cat active both physically and mentally, at whatever level he is capable, for as long as possible, is one of the keys to a long, high-quality life for him.

Get the Ball Rolling

Before you get the ball rolling, however, consult with your vet. This is important if your cat has been diagnosed with any ailment, is overweight or obese, and/or hasn't been doing much in the way of exercise for years beyond trundling to his food dish and jumping in your lap as you both settle on the sofa for an evening in front of the television. As you know from your own experience with exercise regimes, you can do more harm than good to your cat, if in a spurt of enthusiasm and determination, you try to make up for all those couch-potato nights in a single high-speed session of cat-and-mouse.

Exercise Guidelines

All appearances to the contrary, sedentary posturing is not what your cat was designed by nature to do. Your cat was designed to be a mover and a shaker—to jump, pounce, stalk, climb, scratch, play, and prowl. So if your cat, like so many (especially indoor dwellers), does nothing all day but sleep, eat, use the litter pan, and hog your side of the bed and favorite chair, it's time to get him up and put some bounce back into those famously flexible feline feet! Here's how.

Provide a Variety of Toys

For cats, variety is the spice of life. You want to choose toys that serve the various aspects of cat behavior: hunting, capturing and "killing," climbing, and so on. This does not mean you have to lay out a pile of cash at the nearby pet superstore or online pet products retailer. Most cats love nothing better than a balled up piece of aluminum foil, a grocery bag, a straw, the sock you just took off, the daily newspaper tossed on the floor, or a hundred other "freebies."

You'll want to supply your cat with something to climb and claw, so he won't use the furniture or draperies. Myriad designs and sizes of scratching poles and cat "condos" are available for this purpose. Some are quite pricey, however, so again, depending on your budget and DIY skills, you may want to build your own from an old box and carpet remnants.

As a real eye-opener, tempt your cat into action with a catnip toy. A good idea is to bring out the toy just before you leave for the

day—that catnip mouse will have him exercising on his own in no time. When you come home, however, put the toy away, so that he doesn't become immune to its charms.

Motorized toys, too, can get your cat in the mood by acting as real prey—running sporadically around and adding thrills to the chase. And don't forget the "wand" toys—narrow poles with feathers, balls, and other enticing doodads hanging from the end. Watch your cat take to the air after these temptations.

Warm Up to It

Go easy on your out-of-shape cat. Again, first, make sure you know from your vet what he is and isn't capable of doing at this point in his life and health. And once he has been okayed for exercise, start slow—maybe five to ten minutes a day, increasing to twice a day after a week or so. Watch him carefully: if he suddenly stops and is breathing heavily or even panting, it's time to stop.

You might want to set one exercise-play session just before your bedtime, especially if your cat has been keeping you up nights prowling around and vocalizing. In the same way a long

Toy Taboos

When you don't provide your cat with toys of your choosing, chances are he'll find some for himself. This can be highly dangerous. Every vet has stories to tell of the things cats have ingested and had to have removed, sometimes surgically—such as a sewing needle attached to a piece of thread that attracted one cat's attention. Off-limit items include paper clips, rubber bands, tinsel, earrings, safety pins, plastic razors, staples, string, electrical cords, and many others.

walk helps people to sleep, a game of predator-prey will help your cat sleep, possibly with dreams of the hunt running through his head.

Play Mind Games

As important as it is to exercise your cat's body, it's just as vital to keep him mentally stimulated. Says Dr. Goldston, "Mental stimulation greatly improves both the longevity and quality of life of all senior pets." Failure to do so, he adds, leads to a great increase in obsessive-compulsive disorder (OCD), such as obsessively licking a certain area on his front or back legs or abdomen—sometimes until the area is bald or has developed sores. Mental exercise may also help slow the progression of senility, or cognitive dysfunction syndrome (CDS).

In this regard, be innovative—and follow hints from your cat. As a kitten, did he like nothing better than to get inside a paper grocery bag for a game of hide-and-seek? Why not set up a maze of them, and put a catnip mouse in one, to simulate a hunt? Or is your cat fond of boxes? Why not turn one upside down, with a ball or catnip mouse trapped underneath? Have you ever found your cat in the bathtub happily using the cap from your shampoo bottle (or something similar and equally skittish) as the puck in a game of bath hockey? Put

Bored Out of Their Minds

Did you know that lack of exercise and mental stimulation—boredom—is a major cause of behavior problems among felines, large and small? These problems include not just those that annoy us—scratching furniture, vocalizing incessantly, destroying plants, and not using the litter pan—but some that are downright disturbing, such as self-mutilation and obsessive licking. Behaviorists at the world-famous San Diego Zoo have discovered that by offering, on a regular basis, appropriate physical and mental challenges to their Indo-Chinese tigers, these large cats live longer and happier lives and don't display the same obsessive-compulsive disorders as their indoor domestic relatives.

---

something in there deliberately for him to bat around. Ping-Pong balls are ideal kitty-ware, by the way, as they have no bells, bows, or other attachments that can come off and be ingested.

Another favorite idea of a lot of cat owners, especially those who are gone for long hours at a time each day, is to give their cats company in the form of radio, television, or tapes. Some leave the radio turned on low all day; others prefer to set a timer so that one form of media or the other comes on at certain times of the day.

Finally, don't forget to lay on the love. Dr. Goldston says that probably the most effective mental stimulation for elderly pets is when owners take time each day to pet, scratch, rub, talk—just interact with them. (It's good for you, too. Studies have shown that one of the best ways to relieve stress in people is to stroke a cat or dog.)

ATTENDING TO THE OUTER CAT

Throughout the centuries, cats have been described as vain. Part of that reputation comes from their statuesque, even royal, bearing, and part from their innate grooming behavior. Certainly cats give every

THE STORY OF LUCKY: BRUSHING THE CARES AWAY

One hot summer evening, a young couple went out for a ride on a motorcycle to the desert foothills in Tucson, Arizona, to watch the sunset. What they saw instead was not one of nature's wonders, but an example of the worst in human nature. There, under a Palo Verde tree, was a calico kitten, whose long hair had been burned and throat had been cut. Not stopping to wonder who would do such a thing and why, they knew they had to try and save the kitten.

Thanks to the couple's quick action and the heroic efforts of the vet, the kitten (guesstimated to be less than a year old) survived to go home with her Good Samaritans. Inevitably, everyone who heard the story or saw the cat said the same thing: "That cat's lucky to be alive," so, of course, they named her Lucky.

As the couple's family grew—to include three children and a menagerie of dogs—Lucky was always there, but in the background. She seemed to feel safer keeping her distance, for though her hair had grown back beautifully and covered the scars from her attack, she remained cautious of people.

Lucky was an indoor/outdoor cat, and pretty much came and went as she pleased, though she never strayed far from her home base. She kept to her own agenda, and as her human family became busy with their own—especially as the kids joined various sports teams, requiring them to be out most evenings at one playing field or another—attention to Lucky was hit-or-miss. This wasn't due to lack of love or concern, but to lack of time and energy, and to resources: the family lived on a very tight budget, and health care for even its human members was, in most cases, for emergencies only.

Still, with regular meals, a warm lap on a chilly evening, and an occasional swipe with a comb or brush, Lucky flourished for years—and years and years. It wasn't until she was twenty-something that she started to become more reclusive and stopped grooming herself. But it took a while before the couple noticed that her long, silken fur was becoming matted and that her paws were making an odd clicking sound as she walked across the kitchen floor when she went to eat and drink. On closer inspection, they saw that her nails had grown dramatically—around themselves in a spiral. A local humane society staff member cut away the mats and clipped her nails, then showed the couple how to do it in the future, and explained the importance of keeping up with her grooming on a regular basis.

What a difference the grooming regimen made to Lucky's spirit! The daily brushing seemed to perk her up, as much, it seemed, for the attention she was getting from her owners as from how much better it made her feel physically. And with her nails "manicured," it eased her progress to food and drink and, just as important, to her favorite shady spot under the tree in the front yard—where she sometimes yielded graciously to a gentle licking from one of the family dogs.

A year later, Lucky made her exit from the family in much less dramatic fashion than when she entered it, dying quietly in her sleep. She was buried in her favorite resting place, under the tree.

appearance of caring what they look like. But that's the human take on a behavior that has a much more serious basis, one connected to health and bonding practices of cats domestic and wild. And for senior cats, grooming is imperative. At the least, older cats that no longer groom themselves sufficiently and are not helped by their caregivers will become uncomfortable in their own skins; at the worst, they become at greater risk for succumbing to parasite-borne diseases, ear and eye infections, skin and other cancers, and tooth and gum diseases (the latter of which can turn much more serious, even deadly).

Grooming your cat is one of the best ways to catch signs of problems before they turn serious. Your hands-on attention will lead you to discover early: lumps, tumors, or other skin formations; sores and cuts; skin parasites; hair loss; tender body parts; tooth decay and gum discoloration; and dry, cracked footpads or nails. Grooming is also the ideal way to show your cat love and affection—vital ingredients to his sense of well-being.

As with exercise, elderly cats should receive daily attention, especially those with long hair. When you do this on a regular basis, you'll find it doesn't take long to "run a comb through his hair"; and in the long run, you'll save money in health care costs, by catching things early, when they're more easily treatable.

To help you commit to this aspect of your cat's health care regimen, you might want to assemble a grooming kit and assign a time each day (for example, when you sit down to watch to the news every night) to use it.

Grooming kit components:

- *Brush and comb* appropriate for your cat's hair type and length and skin condition. Your vet or a professional groomer can give you guidance. Then spend some time reading labels on the grooming products on the shelves of your favorite pet supply store.

- *Nail clippers.* Pet supply retailers have clippers specially designed for use on a cat's claws, but many people find their own nail clippers work just as well.
- *Scissors,* to cut away matted hair or trapped debris. Those of you with long-haired cats, be on the lookout for dried feces caught in backside hair.
- *Pet-formulated toothbrush and toothpaste.* The human variety causes stomach upset.
- *Cotton balls and baby oil* to wipe the dirt from the inside of your cat's ears and any discharge from around each eye. Never use a cotton swab to poke in your cat's ears or eyes.

Brushing and Combing

Brushing your cat daily is one of the best things you can do for him: you stimulate oil production to the skin; remove dead skin, loose hair, and mats; and keep dander under control. Brush down to the roots, taking care not to be too rough; remember, an older cat's skin is much more sensitive. If your cat has short or thin hair, you won't need to apply as much pressure as for cats with long hair or an

---

Grooming to Go

If you need help grooming your old cat—perhaps he's too fragile or difficult for you to handle alone, or maybe you have your own age-related disability such as arthritis—be aware that many communities across the country today, especially those with large retirement populations, offer mobile grooming services for pets. Some will pick up, groom, and return your cat to you; others will groom him in your home—ideal for geriatric felines whose immune systems are compromised or who are simply change-resistant. Your vet may know of such a service; and, often, these mobile groomers advertise their services in neighborhood newspapers, pet supply retailers, and grocery stores.

---

undercoat. And if your cat has any harmless growths (which you know because your vet told you), such as common fatty tumors called lipomas, be very careful not to aggravate them with the brush, as they can bleed and become infected.

While you're brushing or combing your cat's hair, check his skin for any growths, sores, or cuts. Don't rely on just a visual; run your hands up and down, over and under. If you see or feel something of concern, jot down a note of where exactly you saw or felt it, so that it's easier to relocate when you're in the vet's office.

Bathing

It's something of an old wives' tale that cats don't like to get wet. Truth is, some don't seem to mind a bit. There are even cats that enjoy playing with water; more than one has been known to fall into a toilet bowl in the process. But, in general, it's true that cats don't like to get wet all over, so bathing them is not something many cat owners do on a regular basis, if ever. Certainly, it's best to get them used to the process when they're young; otherwise, you may want to use the services of a professional groomer.

In any case, older cats should be bathed only when necessary, and then with great care, in shallow (three to four inches), lukewarm water, using pet shampoo only (no human products, please). Towel-dry gently (never use a hair dryer, which can irritate already-sensitive skin). If your elderly feline needs a bath—perhaps he's having incontinence problems—and he's never had one before, a sponge bath may be the best option, as it will be less traumatic for him. Using a soft face cloth that has been dipped in warm water (and pet shampoo, if necessary) then wrung out so it is wet but not dripping, gently clean one part of his body at a time. Make sure to wipe away any soap residue, or it will irritate his skin when it dries. And *never* let your cat out of the bathroom until he is *thoroughly* dry; at his age, a chill can quickly turn into something worse.

Teeth and Gums

As you learned in Chapter 3, brushing your cat's teeth and gums is one of the most important steps you can take to ensure your cat's long life and good health. Periodontal disease, left untreated, can lead to tooth loss and, in the worst cases, infection of major organs including the lungs, kidneys, and liver—even the nervous system—and, eventually, to death (more on this in Chapter 6). Sadly, too few pet owners include brushing their cat's teeth and gums as part of their grooming process, making periodontal disease the most common clinical condition in companion animals, according to the American Veterinary Dental College (AVDC).

It's unclear why so many pet owners neglect this aspect of their cat's care; perhaps it seems too unwieldy or uncomfortable a task. But it's very important to learn, especially for older cats. The less often your cat has to be anesthetized for full cleanings or other dental work, the better. You should brush your cat's teeth a minimum of two to three times a week, though daily is best (once a month is not enough!). Once you get the hang of it, it takes only a few minutes. Your vet or veterinary technician can show you the proper way, and

---

National Pet Dental Health Month

Funded by an educational grant from Hill's Pet Nutrition, Inc., the American Veterinary Medical Association (AVMA) and the American Veterinary Dental Society (AVDS) team up each February to launch a consumer awareness campaign, designed to bring attention to the importance of regular dental care for pets.

---

can give you the proper tools. You'll need a pet-formula toothpaste (made to be swallowed, because cats can't spit) and toothbrush. You might need someone to help control your cat at first, if you've never done this before. Here are four simple getting-started guidelines for those who have never gone hand-to-mouth with their cat before:

1. Don't use the toothbrush at first; instead, using your index finger, rub your cat's gums, front to back. To make this more palatable to him, wrap your finger in gauze, then dip it in some broth before you start.
2. Now try it with the toothbrush, inserting it gently under his cheek. Talk quietly to your cat as you go, to calm him. Don't force it, or he'll never become accustomed to the procedure.
3. For the first few attempts, keep the sessions short.
4. If at first you don't succeed, try, try again.

Your vet may recommend you begin feeding your cat a plaque- and tartar-control food, and add an oral hygiene chew to your cat's diet. You might also investigate some of the newer plaque prevention products on the market, which are designed to help slow plaque buildup, which is the beginning of dental disease.

Ears

The moist inner areas of your cat's ears are prime real estate for mites, bacteria, even yeast infections. To prevent such bad guys from moving into the neighborhood, include ear cleaning as part of your grooming procedure. You'll need cotton balls and some ear cleanser from your vet. This is a fairly simple procedure: squeeze a little cleanser into his ear (not too much, or when he shakes his head, as he inevitably will, most of it will end up on you), fold the earflap down, and hold it for a minute or so, then clean up the excess from the backside of the ear and around the perimeter of the outer canal.

(Do not go too deep into the canal, or you risk doing damage by putting bacteria on the express train to the inner ear.)

Nails

You'll have to be attentive to stay on top of your cat's nail care, and when you've neglected it for too long, you'll get clear clues he's due for a pedicure. Two common signs are the telltale clicking sound across a bare floor and snagging in upholdtered furniture and carpeted areas (your cat may be stopped dead in his tracks when one of his claws gets hooked in a carpet loop). Allowed to grow too long, a cat's claws may curl around themselves and can puncture his footpads, causing pain and possibly infection, and limiting his mobility.

Nail clipping is fast and painless—for both of you—once you get the hang of it, and especially if this has been a regular part of your grooming regimen over the years and you're comfortable using pet nail clippers. Your vet or a groomer will be happy to show you how to proceed and how much to cut (just the white tip of each nail, where it begins to curve—never to the quick, the pink area). But for a lot of people, this is something best left to the pros. It doesn't cost a lot, and takes just minutes if you bring your cat to one of the pet superstores with on-site grooming facilities, and have his nails clipped there. Your vet can do it, too, during a checkup; and, certainly, all groomers offer this service.

And while you're "playing footsie" with your cat, be sure to feel gently between his "toes" for anything irregular, such as cuts, growths, or sore spots. Check his pads, too, which tend to get drier as he gets older and are more prone to cracking and infection.

SUMMARY

There is no way to measure the value of the bond you have with your cat. Most people would say they have no words to describe it. As your cat ages, and your involvement in his care becomes more intense, that bond deepens further still. By providing your cat with proper nutrition, appropriate exercise, and regular grooming, you will be solidifying that bond at the same time you are ensuring a high quality of life for him.

KEY PET POINTS

- With guidance from your vet, shop carefully for your cat's food. Do not be penny-wise and pound-foolish: cheaper food is almost always of poorer quality, and you'll pay for it in the long run when you have to address diet-related health problems in your cat.
- Keeping your cat active, both physically and mentally, is essential for his well-being over the long term. There are exercise options and toys galore today that can make this fun for both of you.
- Proper grooming (including brushing his teeth) not only makes your cat feel good and look good, it's one of the best ways to keep him in good health. It also helps you to stay on top of any changes to his body, so that they can be addressed early, when treatment options are most effective.
- Always follow your vet's recommendations for feeding, exercising, and grooming your cat. Too much is at stake to do otherwise.

CHAPTER 6

When Your Cat Gets Sick: Understanding Common Age-Related Ailments and Their Treatments

Age is not a disease. Veterinary practitioners, schools, and organizations are unanimous in making that point. Further, they stress that age itself must be distinguished from the physiologic changes that come with the aging process. That may sound like a medical runaround, but it's not. And it's worth taking the time to understand what may seem like a subtle distinction. As cats age, their bodies reflect that process in a number of ways (just like us). Some age better, that is, more slowly and/or with fewer obvious or detrimental changes (again, just like us). They get sick, some more seriously than others, some sooner rather than later. In their joint publication, "Panel Report on Feline Senior Care," the American Association of Feline Practitioners (AAFP) and the Academy of Feline Medicine (AFM) report that, "Changes in senior cats occur across a fairly wide age range. While many cats begin to show clinically significant changes between seven and ten years of age, most do so by twelve years of age." Another factor contributing to the health of a senior cat is that, according to the report, "geriatric disorders tend to be

chronic and progressive," and "the senior patient is more likely to experience multiple medical problems simultaneously." So, in sum, though old age is not a disease, disease is a virtually inevitable side effect of aging. What is required of you, the devoted companion to a senior cat, is the careful monitoring of your cat's health status, as described in Chapter 4 on wellness programs, and understanding, if only peripherally, of the various illnesses, diseases, and ailments common to the senior cat.

Helping you achieve the second objective is the goal of this chapter. It includes a brief overview of a number of the ailments prevalent among the senior and geriatric cat population. The keyword here is "brief": the intent of this information is to familiarize you with a number of the most common age-related changes your cat may experience; it is not meant to serve as a means of diagnosis. If your cat is showing signs that all is not well or "right," only a qualified veterinarian can and should diagnose your cat.

Admittedly, a list of disease descriptions hardly makes for pleasurable reading, so you might want to just skim through these sections, taking special note of the symptoms given in the "At a Glance" boxes. If something raises a red flag, read more closely; if you're still concerned, call your vet. Don't jump to conclusions. The objective here is to become informed, so that you can proceed appropriately.

Looks Can Be Deceiving

As your knowledge of age-related feline illness grows, don't let it overshadow your instincts where your cat is concerned. Remember, cats are masters of disguise when it comes to illness, and they can look healthy until a disease or ailment has become very serious. Subtle signs (including your own "hunches") are important to follow when it comes to the health of your elderly cat.

Most important, as you read about what can go wrong, keep in mind that advances in veterinary medicine can, in many cases, help things go right again—no, not forever, but for longer than previously possible. Today's veterinarians and veterinary specialists can routinely offer treatments that, not too long ago, were reserved only for the human animal—including pacemakers, kidney transplants, radiation and chemotherapy, sophisticated testing protocols, and much, much more. (Of course, these high-level treatments come at a price, a health care issue we'll address in the next chapter.)

CHOOSING TREATMENT PROTOCOLS

In reading about these age-related diseases and conditions, you'll note in many cases that more than one type of treatment may be appropriate. It will be up to you, the pet owner, in close consultation with your vet, to decide how to proceed. A number of factors will go into your decision-making process, which will include:

- Your cat's specific diagnosis
- Her prognosis (her prospect of recovery) and her quality of life as a sick cat
- Your health care preferences (Do you tend to have faith in the latest drug treatments, for example, or do you prefer to take an alternative approach, such as acupuncture, if one's available and appropriate?)
- The cost of the recommended treatment and your budget (Can you afford it?)
- The amount and type of care required of you (Do you have the time? Are you prepared to give shots, clean wounds, deal with drug side effects, and so on, possibly for an extended period of time?)

There may be other factors, based on your individual lifestyle and circumstances. In its "Senior Care Guidelines for Dogs and Cats," the American Animal Hospital Association (AAHA) recommends that its member veterinarians always tell their clients all the best options, even those the vet believes the client will decline. "The veterinarian," the guidelines state, "has a responsibility to *recommend* what is best for the pet, but the *chosen* treatment must be what is best for both the patient and the client." To that end, your vet should:

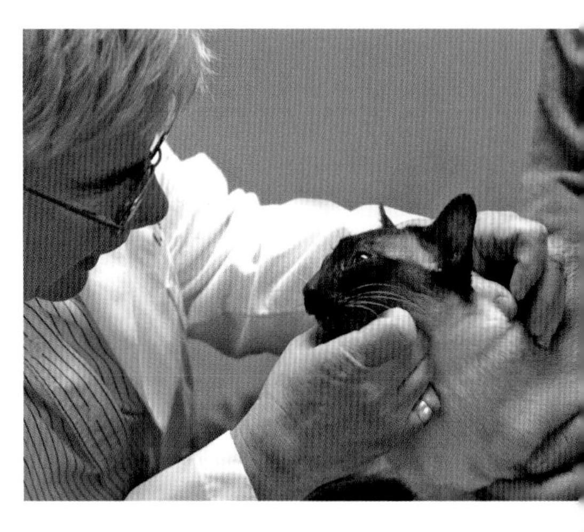

1. Explain all the consequences of each available choice, including your responsibilities and all related costs in time and money.
2. Design a treatment protocol that best enables you to comply with it. (Will you be able to administer twice-daily shots to your diabetic cat, for example, or give daily subcutaneous injections to your cat in renal failure? If not, alternative approaches should be discussed, as well as talking about what will happen if you choose to do nothing.)
3. Detail all side effects and quality-of-life issues associated with the treatment of choice.
4. Back up verbal instructions with clear written documentation, and offer training, if necessary, in treatment delivery.
5. Explain how to monitor your cat's response to the chosen treatment. (Typically, you will be asked to log any side effects or complications you notice, including behavioral changes. Keeping a written log is especially important if your cat is taking more than one medication, when drug interactions must be closely tracked. Doing so will help your vet adjust dosage, or switch or discontinue drugs.)

Tip: Keep a Treatment Log

A small notebook is good for treatment tracking. A memo calendar is even better, in which you can note the dates of treatments, along with your cat's reactions and responses. Keep the calendar in the same place you keep your cat's medications or other treatment instructions, to remind you to update it. And when you check in with your vet by phone, e-mail, or in person, have the calendar in hand.

It is when your cat is sick that your partnership with your vet becomes the most meaningful. To give your cat the best care available, your vet will be counting on you to supply the information necessary to provide that level of care. This is why it is so important to establish a rapport with your vet early on, during wellness checkups. Looking for the right vet when your cat is already ill will only add stress (remember the stories of Boodie and Sunshine?).

Types of Treatment: Definition of Terms

In the next section, which describes a number of conditions common to aging cats, you'll see in many cases more than one type of treatment listed. Some are considered traditional, others alternative. It's important to understand what those terms mean in a medical context.

"Traditional" is the word used by health care practitioners and consumers alike to mean the established or customary way of treating illness and disease, as taught in most medical school curricula in this country. Traditional medicine includes various testing and exploratory procedures for diagnostic purposes, surgeries, therapeutic drug treatments, and so on.

In addition to traditional approaches, a number of alternative treatment choices are available to pet owners and veterinary practitioners. Most of these are options also available in human health care.

In the context of medical care, "alternative" just means "another," "unconventional," or "nonstandard." It does not mean not as good; it just means different. Whether an alternative choice for medical treatment is better or worse than a traditional approach depends on a number of factors: the medical condition being treated, the professional delivering the treatment, whether other treatments are being given, at what stage during the disease or illness treatment began, and many others. But the same potential for success exists whether you choose a traditional or alternative treatment method for your cat.

The term "alternative medicine" came into use around 1977 to describe various systems of healing or treating disease. It is usually thought to include acupuncture, traditional Chinese medicine (TCM), chiropractic, homeopathy, herbal treatments, faith healing, and others. Typically, these methods are not included in the traditional medical curricula taught in the United States, though this has been changing slowly in recent years. Interestingly, some alternative treatments, such as acupuncture, have been in use thousands of years longer than so-called traditional medicine.

Finally, there's "integrative medicine," a newer term in the medical lexicon. It simply means to coordinate, incorporate, or blend two or more treatment options into a protocol as appropriate for a given condition and a given patient. This is the approach favored by many veterinary practitioners today. Dr. Goldston says, "The ideal

---

Give Me an Alternative

If you are interested in learning more about alternative approaches to traditional veterinary practice or want to find a vet specializing in alternative and holistic treatments, go to www.alternativesfor animals.com. In addition to a directory of prescreened vets and practitioners, you'll find links there for natural foods and supplements, animal communicators and pet psychics, and much more.

Call for Regulation

Though Dr. Goldston believes there is a place for holistic medicine in animal care, a major problem he sees is that, currently, there are no regulations in place to ensure the purity and volume of active ingredients in holistic medicines, as there are for traditional medications. Alternative medicines are considered dietary or nutritional supplements or nutrients, not pharmaceuticals, and there are no federal or state regulatory bodies such as the Federal Drug Administration (FDA) or the United States Department of Agriculture (USDA) to monitor content claims.

situation to me is definitely an integrative approach. The only definite wrong to me is to only rely on conventional veterinary medicine *or* alternative veterinary medicine 100 percent of the time."

You as a pet owner have access to all these forms of treatment for your cat. Which you choose will depend on your understanding of the approach that has the best chance of success, your preferences for or against traditional versus alternative treatments, cost, and so on.

DISEASES AND CONDITIONS COMMON AMONG AGING CATS

The list of diseases and conditions given here is far from comprehensive; as stated, it is intended only to introduce you to a number of the health issues your cat may face as she ages. And, again, this material is

Contact Point

For more information on animal acupuncture, and to find a specialist in your area, go to the American Holistic Veterinary Medical Association (AHVMA) Web site: www.ahvma.org.

supplied only for informational purposes: only a certified veterinarian, performing the requisite exams and tests, can properly diagnose and treat a sick animal. If your cat is displaying symptoms of illness of any kind, make an appointment with your vet as soon as possible.

By the Letter

For convenience, the diseases and conditions listed in this section are given in alphabetical order.

Arthritis

As it is among the human population, this degenerative joint and cartilage disease is very common in aging cats, making it painful for them to walk and jump—in general, move. Quality of life can become seriously impaired, as your cat becomes increasingly restricted from interacting in any kind of meaningful way. Caused in most cases by simple wear to bones and joints over time, arthritis often manifests at points of previous injury or where there's a history of infection. In most cases, senior cats (some middle-aged ones, too) will develop *osteoarthritis*, the degeneration of cartilage covering the

AT A GLANCE: ARTHRITIS

Symptoms	Diagnosis	Treatment(s)
Stiffness; difficulty getting up and down; limping or favoring one side; vocalizing or yowling on sudden movement; licking sore limb/joint	Physical exam of affected limb(s); possibly X-rays	Nonsteroidal anti-inflammatory drugs (NSAIDs); neutraceuticals such as glucosamine and chondroitin sulfate; acupuncture, massage; dietary adjustments, especially to reduce weight and weight-induced pressure on affected limbs/joints; surgery

ends of the bones, as opposed to *rheumatoid arthritis*, an autoimmune condition where the body attacks its own joints and tissues.

Keeping your cat in shape through regular exercise and proper nutrition are your best lines of defense against this painful disease, as well as after your cat has been diagnosed (see Chapter 5). When it comes to treatment, many pet owners and vets take a truly integrative approach, combining prescription medications such as non-steroidal anti-inflammatory drugs (NSAIDs) with supplements and alternative treatments, most popular among them being acupuncture. Or they may switch between them, as the effectiveness of one begins to wear off.

Reminder

Never, never, never give your cat aspirin, acetaminophen (e.g., Tylenol), or ibuprofen (e.g., Motrin) to treat arthritis pain. Though widely used by humans to ease discomfort from this debilitating disease, these drugs are lethal to cats.

Cancer

It's the dreaded "C word," the one every pet owner hopes they never will hear. Unfortunately, reports the American Veterinary Medical Association (AVMA), cancer is responsible for almost half the deaths in pets over ten years of age (dogs get cancer more often than cats). But, today, cancer does not automatically mean a death sentence. As in humans, some feline cancers can be cured, others managed to extend life and offer quality of life. Though all cancers have in common abnormal, uncontrollable cell growth that invades and destroys normal, healthy tissue, cancer is not a single disease. It takes many forms, some more dangerous than others.

In most cases, the causes of feline cancer are unknown, but as in the human population there are some likely triggers: a genetic predisposition and exposure to elements that provoke cell abnormalities, such as carcinogenic (cancer-causing) chemicals and sunlight. It is also known that some viral infections in cats cause cancer. The most well known of these is feline leukemia, which, thanks to vaccinations, is less common than it once was. Ironically, however, vaccinations themselves are believed to be the cause of another form of cancer in cats, called *sarcoma*, which develops at injection sites. This is why, as explained in Chapter 4, your cat's vaccination protocol must be evaluated carefully by your vet, based on her age, health status, risk of exposure, and other relevant factors.

AT A GLANCE: CANCER, GENERALLY

Symptoms	Diagnosis	Treatment(s)
Abnormal swellings or growths; sores that don't heal; weakness, shortness of breath, or difficulty breathing; difficulty eating or swallowing, loss of appetite, or weight loss; bleeding or discharge from any body openings; problems urinating/defecating	Depending on the symptoms: aspiration and/or biopsy, for external growths; imaging tools such as X-rays, ultrasound, or magnetic resonance imaging (MRI); exploratory surgery for internal tumors; consultation with veterinary oncologist (cancer specialist)	Depending on the diagnosis: surgery, chemotherapy, radiation; nutritional and holistic therapies

Some of the cancers prevalent among aging and geriatric cats include the following:

- *Lymphoma.* Lymphoma, probably the most common cancer to develop in cats, is a rapidly growing malignancy of the body's lymph system, which includes virtually every organ in the body. The first sign is one or more suspicious lumps, with no accompanying symptoms of illness. Diagnosis typically involves a physical exam of the lump(s), blood tests and a urinalysis, and biopsy or aspiration of one or more lymph nodes. Lymphoma is a "staged" disease, meaning it is classified in stages of severity, in this case I through V with Stage I being the least severe. Early-stage lymphoma can be managed for months or longer with chemotherapy.

- *Osteosarcoma.* This is bone cancer, typically affecting the limbs and spine. It is a fast-spreading tumor, which by the time it has been found is considered to have already spread. Unchecked, it metastasizes (spreads) to the lungs and lymph nodes. Primary signs are lameness and tenderness of the affected area, which become progressively worse as the disease develops, causing severe pain. X-rays are used for diagnosis, or a tiny section of bone can be removed for laboratory analysis. In some cases, the recommended treatment is amputation of the affected bone, followed by chemotherapy or radiation to limit the spread of any cancer cells.
- *Mammary (breast) cancer.* This cancer is most commonly seen in unspayed female cats, and 85 percent of breast tumors in cats are malignant. The keyword here is "unspayed." Spaying your cat when she is between six and twelve months old will greatly reduce her chances of developing this deadly cancer. The primary sign to watch for is a lump or lumps in the mammary glands that are firm to the touch, especially in the area of the back legs. Many of these tumors will be found to be benign, but they all must be tested, as early treatment of small tumors is generally more successful than for multiple or large growths. Testing may be done preliminarily through needle aspiration, used to

---

Spay to Prevent Cancer

Even if your older cat is in a high-risk group for breast cancer (she's older, unspayed, and has had kittens), it doesn't mean you shouldn't have her spayed now. Spaying at any age can help prevent tumor formation.

---

withdraw some cells from the growth for lab evaluation, and ultimately via a biopsy to confirm diagnosis.

- *Squamous cell carcinoma.* This is a skin cancer, caused by exposure to the sun, and is more common among outdoor cats, especially those with white fur or living in hot sunny climates. Fortunately, caught early, these cancerous growths can be surgically removed or treated with radiation therapy or cryosurgery (freezing the tumor with liquid nitrogen).
- *Oral squamous cell carcinoma.* This cancer develops in the cells lining the mouth or throat, and often involves the tongue. It causes progressive difficulty with eating, seriously bad breath, drooling, and loss of appetite. This type of cancer is very difficult to treat.

This list is far from comprehensive, as there are numerous different types and manifestations of cancer, just as in the human population and in other animals.

Cancer Treatments

The most widely used cancer treatments are surgery, chemotherapy, radiation, and, in a supporting role, nutrition.

- *Surgery.* Sometimes invasive treatments are performed to partially or entirely remove a cancerous tumor or other malignant growth, depending on its location. Surgery is often supplemented with chemotherapy or radiation, for insurance or to attack cancer cells that could not be removed surgically.
- *Chemotherapy.* This is, simply, drug therapy, as opposed to surgery or radiation. Powerful drugs are administered in a series to kill cancer cells or slow their growth. It is important to note that animals typically do not suffer the serious side effects of chemotherapy that humans do. Few suffer hair loss (though some lose their whiskers) and few develop infection or experience nausea, and rarely do they have to be hospitalized due to side

Anesthetizing the Older Cat

Thanks to new types of anesthesia and procedures, it is safer today than in the past to anesthetize old and/or sick cats, but it is still a risky business, one that must be approached with caution. Your vet will give your cat a thorough workup to determine whether she is strong enough to be anesthetized.

Before agreeing to any procedure that will require your cat to be anesthetized, make sure your vet explains in detail all the risks involved, as well as the benefits. As for human patients, veterinarians will ask you to sign "informed consent" forms for all procedures.

effects of the medications. Older cats, however, generally have lower tolerance to these powerful drugs.

- *Radiation.* The objective of radiation is to aim powerful X-rays at the cancerous growth or area, ideally sparing the healthy tissue around it. Typically, radiation is used for cases of inoperable cancers or to supplement surgery. Cats receiving this form of treatment may develop soreness in their mouth, making it difficult for them to eat, just when they need nutrition most.
- *Nutritional therapy.* Loss of appetite is common among feline cancer patients, and weight loss and corresponding weakness can seriously affect how well they respond to their primary cancer treatment. It is important, therefore, to talk to your vet about special diets, supplements, and ways to tempt your cat to eat while she's undergoing treatment for cancer.

Cancer Information and Support

Sadly, cancer is one of the most commonly diagnosed diseases in senior cats, especially in those over ten. The good news is there's an abundance of information and support available. In addition to consultations with your vet and, if called for, a veterinary oncologist (cancer specialist), you may want to do further research on your own, or connect with other pet owners whose cats have cancer. Two good places to start are:

- Veterinary Cancer Society: www.vetcancersociety.org
- Perseus Foundation: www.perseusfoundation.org

THE STORY OF TOMMY AND BABETTE: A TALE OF TWO KITTIES

For my ninth birthday, more than anything I wanted a puppy. But my mother was not thrilled with the idea of giving me a dog, because she knew the burden of its care would fall on her shoulders. (She had spent the previous summer caring for the rat and gerbils I'd volunteered to watch for school; and neither I nor my dad, who worked late hours, was going to be riding the elevator at 11:00 p.m. to take a puppy out for a last walk.) So what I got instead was Tommy. Almost as if on cue, a few days before my birthday, my mother found a black, six-week-old ball of fluff that had been left abandoned on the street. He meowed; she picked him up, brought him home, and introduced me to my new pet.

At first I was disappointed, but pretty quickly I was dressing up Tommy in frilly doll clothes and tossing him balls to chase across the living room floor. Tommy was truly one of the family, and he played no favorites; he belonged to all of us equally. He would sit on Mom's lap for hours as she read the paper or played solitaire; chase dad's shoelaces; and eat Grandma's cooking, which the rest of us were reluctant to do (for his loyalty, Tommy was rewarded with fresh fish, cooked to order). Most important, he was just my friend. We grew up together, and he was there when others were no longer, for he outlived both my grandmother and my mother, seeing me effectively through my childhood. And for all those years, he lived a healthy life—until he was about sixteen.

At that time, the vet explained to me that Tommy was old but not dying. And in his case, old age meant his kidneys were starting to fail and that he would need help in the form of injections of fluid under his skin to keep his kidneys functioning. That meant purchasing saline solution, needles, and tubing, and performing a twice-daily process that would take approximately fifteen minutes each time. I worried: Could I do it? Was I willing to make that commitment until the treatment ceased to be effective? If the answer to either of those questions was no, I knew it would be kinder to let him go. Looking at my oldest friend, I answered my own questions with another: How could I not?

Tommy: Girl's best friend

We had another three wonderful years together, and I came to value our treatment time as a bonding experience. For a while, Tommy endured it stoically, probably as another human quirk; but eventually he tired of being pricked, and would hide when treatment time came. Then, as the vet told me it would, the time came when the treatments were not enough. Tommy lost his appetite, became skinnier, and spent most of his time sleeping or hiding. I knew the time was coming when I would have to make the toughest decision of my life. The morning I found him covered in his own fecal matter I knew it was time to let him go—I was keeping him around more for me than for him.

The day I took him to be euthanized, the vet gave me the option of being in the room when the injection was given, and so I held Tommy as he went to sleep for the last time. He passed with a quiet sigh. I pet him one last time, marveling how small he now was and how soft his fur still felt. And though I was heartbroken, I was at peace with my decision.

A couple of years later I met Babette at the Humane Society. She could not have been more different from my quiet, easy-going Tommy. This was a calico with attitude, and then some. And she had the track record to prove it: she had been returned several times, earning the notation on her record as "unmanageable." And if I doubted it, the first time I touched her, she drew blood. But something clicked and I took her home with me that day.

Named Elizabeth by the shelter, she became Babette upon entering my house. Oblivious to the fact that she probably was getting her last chance at a good home, she remained regal, finicky, and unrepentant—she would suffer being touched only on her terms. The unwary or unbelieving who trespassed her personal space would get a sharp, to-the-point message; she was, simply, a sharp-clawed diva.

But we got along famously; she was a one-woman cat and that woman was me. Granted, I sported some impressive scars from our wrestling matches but I didn't care. Babette took no guff from life and taught me to do the same.

Unlike Tommy, though, Babette was already older when I got her and she had been spayed late, which I later learned made her more susceptible to certain diseases. And, sure enough, one day as I was rubbing her belly I felt a lump in one of her breasts. A trip to the vet confirmed she had developed mammary tumors. She had surgery, but

within two years the tumors came back. I agreed to a second operation, but this time her vulnerability was apparent. She showed fear for the first time and, I think, as a result, did not come out of it as well. There was still a fire alight in her spirit but her body could not warm to it.

I started to wonder what would happen if the tumors came back again. Could I, would I, put her through a third operation? Was that fair? The visits to the vet frightened her and stressed her out. Would I be doing more harm than good? Was she in pain? How could I be sure? Even if it meant she might live a few months longer, was it worth it if she had a reduced quality of life? Quality or quantity...? Each day I watched her for a sign, and one day I got it: the tumors had come back.

I opted not to put her through a third operation, and instead began worrying and watching her like a hawk, so that I would know when it was time to let her go. For several months she was almost her old wild self; then, one morning a few days before Christmas, I woke to find her panting, and she looked like she was in pain. I called the vet immediately, to say I was bringing her in—though I found myself wrestling with my decision even as I jumped quickly in the shower.

In the end, though, my on-her-own-terms cat made the decision for me, for when I came out of the shower, Babette was gone. In those few minutes, she had passed, in her own way, in her own home—on her own. I was devastated I hadn't been with her, but I think that's how she wanted it.

We buried her later that morning, while a cold rain was falling. It was late December, and the ground was partially frozen; and because, in dying, she had stretched herself out full length, we had to make a large hole, which took hours of chopping through the hard, icy mix. I like to think it was her way of getting the last word in.

Micheline Frederick, New York

Cognitive Dysfunction Syndrome (CDS)

Cognitive dysfunction syndrome, likened to Alzheimer's disease in humans, has been widely described in dogs but less so in cats. It is manifested by very disturbing behavioral changes that cannot be attributed to any medical problem. Suddenly your cat just doesn't seem like your cat anymore: a sweet-natured companion may become uncharacteristically aggressive toward you, other members of the household, or visitors; she may be unable to sleep, and wander and/or "talk" ceaselessly, often throughout the night; and she ignores the litter pan in favor of your plants, sofa cushions, or the bath mat.

AT A GLANCE: COGNITIVE DYSFUNCTION SYNDROME

Symptoms	Diagnosis	Treatment(s)
Disorientation or confusion; change in litter box habits; sleeplessness; restlessness; uncharacteristic aggression or anxiety; increased vocalizing at higher volume	Thorough exam, to rule out underlying medical problem as cause of behavior changes	Regular physical and mental exercise; nutritional therapy; consistent interaction with members of the household

Although there is a CDS drug treatment now approved for use in dogs, and it is showing good results; at the time of this writing it has not been approved for cats, so proper nutrition and an appropriate exercise program are your only hopes for slowing the progression of this upsetting syndrome.

Dental Disease

Feline periodontal disease is the result of poor or absent dental care. It begins when plaque (formed when bacteria multiply on the teeth and gums) mixes over time with saliva and it hardens to make tartar and calculus. These substances then irritate the gums, which turn red and tender, a stage called gingivitis. Left unchecked, gingivitis causes the gums to eventually begin to separate from the teeth, forming pockets for more bacteria and food particles. Finally, the bacteria attack the roots of the teeth and bone tissue in the jaw. Your cat now will probably be in pain; her gums may bleed; she'll have bad breath and trouble eating.

Worse may be yet to come. If still left untreated, the bacteria may enter the bloodstream, a highway to the major organs, potentially infecting the heart, kidneys, lungs, and liver. Left unaddressed, periodontal disease can damage your cat's major organs and can even cause death.

AT A GLANCE: PERIODONTAL DISEASE

Symptoms	Diagnosis	Treatment(s)
Bad breath and yellow, crusty teeth; trouble eating, especially dry, hard food; swollen, red, or bleeding gums; loose teeth	Full physical exam and medical history; exam of mouth, teeth, and gums; possibly blood and other diagnostic tests to evaluate status of major organs	Professional cleaning, with recommendations for regular dental home care; potential switch to tartar- or plaque-control cat food

Certain breeds of cats whose upper jaw is shorter than their lower, such as the Persian, are at greater risk because their teeth are crowded into a much smaller mouth, making them more prone to plaque buildup and ensuing gingivitis.

Conscientious dental care (see Chapter 5), at home and professionally, is the only way to prevent periodontal disease.

Diabetes Mellitus

Diabetes mellitus (sugar diabetes) is caused by the failure of your cat's pancreas to properly produce insulin, the hormone that helps the body process blood sugar. There are two types of diabetes, Type I and Type II; the first is both more serious and more common in cats—accounting for 50 to 70 percent of diagnoses.

Type I diabetes, also called insulin-dependent diabetes, has no cure. The pancreas fails to produce insulin at all, and so the disease is managed by the administration of insulin, most typically through injection. Type II diabetes has the opposite manifestation: the pancreas produces too much insulin. It is caused primarily from a poor

AT A GLANCE: DIABETES MELLITUS

Symptoms	Diagnosis	Treatment(s)
Insatiable thirst and increased urination; weight loss though appetite has increased; eye cloudiness	Blood and urine tests	Primarily insulin injections; medication to lower the blood glucose concentration; dietary management; exercise

diet of too many carbohydrates over a long period of time; and, not surprisingly, obesity is strongly implicated in this form of the disease. Often, Type II can be treated with a weight loss, exercise, and diet regimen, though medication may be necessary, too.

The contrast between the two types ends there, for the result is the same: blood sugar levels that are too high. Hence, both types require medical intervention and careful monitoring, as each can lead to kidney damage, coma, blindness, and death.

Watch especially for significantly increased water consumption coupled with increased urination. Also be aware that your cat may seem to be eating heartily and more often, yet still be losing weight.

Most cats diagnosed with Type I diabetes will require insulin injections, usually twice a day, although some can be maintained on once-daily injections. Close monitoring by your veterinarian will be necessary to ensure that the dose of insulin remains at the proper level to maintain optimal blood glucose concentration. If the dose is too low, serious illness usually results; if the dose is too high, it can cause seizures and death.

Effective diets for diabetes are now widely available, but do not begin this nutritional regimen without the go-ahead from your vet. In many cases, you'll be given a prescription diet available only from a vet's office. And, typically, you'll be required to feed your cat twice daily to coordinate with the insulin injections.

Having a Seizure

Though cats of any age may experience seizures, older cats are more prone to them. There are a number of possible causes: trauma or infection, low blood sugar, hyperthyroidism, toxins in the blood, external poisons, or a tumor growing off the skull and pressing on the brain. Blood tests are usually run first to confirm or rule out various types of seizures. When a brain tumor is suspected, a CAT scan or MRI is usually recommended. These tumors often are operable if found early.

Seizure behavior is not the same in all cases. Some cats will fall to the floor, writhing and foaming at the mouth, legs flailing in the air; others will assume a "slumping" posture—head down and tail between legs—and whimper or yowl; still others will run around wildly, as if trying to escape their own bodies. Often the eyes will bulge and the cat will bite her tongue.

If your cat has a seizure, take her to a vet as soon as it is over.

Ear Infections

What is more mesmerizing than feline ears? They can rotate independently 180 degrees and be aimed one at a time or both in the direction of any sound the cat hears. The outer ear alone is controlled by thirty-plus muscles (ours have six each); and, working together, the various parts of a cat's ears enable them to hear very high frequencies, from approximately 30 hertz to 60 kilohertz (humans can hear in the approximate range of 20 hertz to 20

AT A GLANCE: EAR INFECTIONS

Symptoms	Diagnosis	Treatment(s)
Discharge, especially dark and waxy, bloody, or puslike; frequent scratching or head shaking; inflammation; odor	Exam of discharge for mites; culture, to detect type of bacteria or yeast	Cleaning, by vet, to remove wax and other discharge; regimen of drops and possibly antibiotics, depending on diagnosis

kilohertz; dogs, 20 hertz to 40 kilohertz). Their ears are an essential component to the makeup of nature's perfect predator.

But a cat's ears are also highly sensitive to infections, caused by mites, bacteria, or yeast cells, especially if she has a weakened ear canal due to allergies, previous infections or injury, and even wetness.

The best preventive measure is cleanliness—with a big *but*. Do not be overzealous in your efforts and go too deep into your cat's ears. The best way to clean your cat's ears is the one your vet has demonstrated for you.

Eye Diseases

Much has been written about the sphinxlike quality of a cat's eyes, but words fail to capture their magnetic effect. One can only stare in wonder. It is not surprising then that, for many cat owners, the first sign they notice as their cats grow older is in their eyes—usually a milkiness or cloudiness. Here again, the caution against attributing any change in your cat's appearance to "just old age" holds, for senior cats are prone to a number of eye illnesses, two of them common to their human companions and just as potentially devastating: cataracts and glaucoma.

CATARACTS

A cataract, an opacity or cloudiness in the lens of the eye, usually occurs with age, though it may have many other causes: congenital,

AT A GLANCE: CATARACTS

Symptoms	Diagnosis	Treatment(s)
Corneal cloudiness, usually blue-gray in color; if advanced, apparent blindness	Eye exam; blood tests to check for underlying cause; possibly ultrasound	Surgery or dissolution of the cataract; eye drops

other age-related illness, trauma, dietary deficiency, or disease-related condition (in particular, diabetes). The cat with cataracts is unable to see through the cloudy part of the lens, and if the entire lens is involved, the cat will be blind in that eye, or completely blind when both eyes are affected.

Also be aware that a much less serious condition, *nuclear sclerosis*, may be mistaken for cataracts. This is not a disease, but an age-related condition that does not cause blindness. Only a veterinary ophthalmologist can tell the difference, through an eye exam.

The standard cataract treatment is surgical removal or dissolution of the cataract, but this is not recommended (it is invasive and expensive) unless your cat is in good health otherwise, she has cataracts in both eyes, and there is hope of restoring vision. (If your cat has vision in one eye, surgery is not recommended.) Following surgery, you will have to administer eye drops.

GLAUCOMA

Glaucoma is increased pressure within the eye, caused when the clear fluid that maintains the shape of the eye and nourishes the eye tissues can no longer drain properly, resulting in a buildup of pressure in the eye. This in turn causes the eye to stretch and enlarge.

Cats get glaucoma much less frequently than dogs; and it is very nearly always secondary to another health problem. To determine whether your cat has glaucoma, your vet will measure the pressure in her eyes (just as your eye doctor does for you), as well as perform other tests to check for underlying causes.

It's important to repeat that cats are expert at hiding signs of illness or discomfort, and eye disease in cats can be especially tricky to identify because the signs may mimic those of many other problems. If you notice red or bloodshot eyes and/or a cloudy cornea, don't wait to take your cat in for a workup, for treatment type and effectiveness depend on the stage of the disease at the time of diagnosis.

AT A GLANCE: GLAUCOMA

Symptoms	Diagnosis	Treatment(s)
Redness around the rim; bloodshot eyes; also, listlessness, decreased appetite; irritability	Pressure tests; others, to determine underlying cause	Early stage: eye drops or drugs; later: surgery

Other Eye Conditions

In addition to the aforementioned nuclear sclerosis, your cat may also develop conjunctivitis ("pinkeye"), an inflammation that has many potential causes: irritation or abrasion; bacterial, fungal, or viral infections; allergies; and others. If your cat has conjunctivitis, you may see her pawing at her eye, and there may be redness and discharge. After attempting to isolate the cause (not always possible), your vet may prescribe an eye ointment, an antibiotic or a corticosteroid (or both), to clear up the infection and reduce irritation. Two important notes:

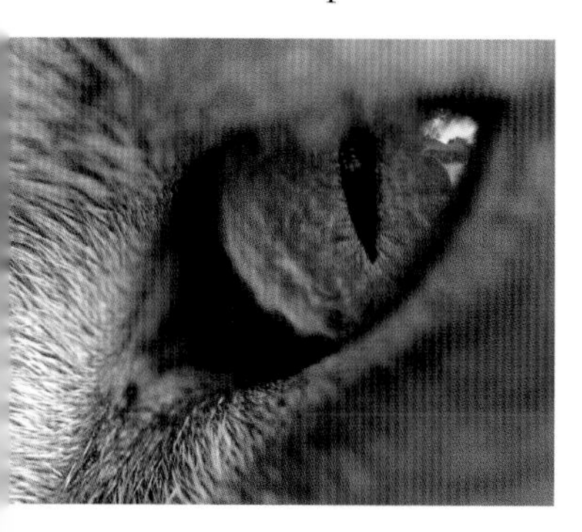

First, conjunctivitis is highly contagious between cats, so if you have more than one, keep them separated until the affected cat has been treated successfully; and if yours is an outdoor cat, keep her indoors for the duration of the treatment period. Second, it may be chronic, owing to a herpes viral infection, in which case, it may return again and again.

Aging cats also commonly develop what's called, simply, "dry eye"—when the eye fails to produce enough tears to moisten and bathe the eye. In addition to age, allergies may be the cause; or it may occur as a side effect of medication your cat is taking. Redness and discharge are usually obvious signs of dry eye. Treatment is usually in the form of an eye ointment to increase tear production, or artificial tears. (Note: *Never* give your cat over-the-counter human versions of these products.) You'll also help to make your cat more comfortable by keeping her hair trimmed around the eyes and by cleaning the eye area regularly, with gauze or a cotton ball saturated with warm water.

Special Treatment

Many veterinarians today limit the scope of their practice to one discipline, such as surgery or oncology (the study of tumors). That means you have access to highly trained experts in many fields, from cardiology, ophthalmology, dermatology, anesthesiology, nutrition, acupuncture, and many others.

According to the AVMA, a veterinary specialist is a graduate veterinarian who has successfully completed the process of board certification in an AVMA-recognized veterinary specialty organization. This requires extensive postgraduate training and experience, a credentials review, and examinations set by the given specialty organization.

Heart Disease

Feline heart disease usually takes the form of diseases of the heart muscle. Called *cardiomyopathy* (*cardio*, meaning "heart"; *myo*, "muscle"; and *pathy*, "disease"), cats may get three types:

- *Hypertrophic cardiomyopathy (HCM)*. This is by far the most common feline heart disease, but it affects mostly younger cats.

Areas of the heart muscle (the left ventricle, usually) grow and thicken.

- *Dilatative cardiomyopathy (DCM).* This type of heart disease is marked by enlarged heart chambers caused by weakening of the heart muscle. DCM is rarely seen today, thanks to the addition of taurine in most quality brands of cat food.
- *Restrictive cardiomyopathy (RCM).* Similar to HCM, this form of cardiomyopathy is more common in older than younger cats. Cats with RCM have hearts with reduced capability to pump, causing an accumulation of blood in the heart and enlargement of the atrium.

In addition to these three cardiomyopathies, and despite advances in their treatments, a common and dangerous complication of feline heart disease is *arterial thromboembolism*, when a blood clot (thrombus) forms in the heart, then breaks away and travels through the bloodstream, eventually lodging in a blood vessel somewhere else in the body (often, in the back legs).

What is particularly devastating about feline heart disease is that early detection is only possible through regular checkups, as generally there are no symptoms in the early stages. Later, your cat will have coughing spells, increased heart rate or arrhythmia (irregular

AT A GLANCE: HEART DISEASE, GENERALLY

Symptoms	Diagnosis	Treatment(s)
None at early stages. Later: coughing or difficulty breathing; weakness and lethargy. Late-stage: difficulty breathing even at rest; loss of appetite and corresponding weight loss; extreme weakness; leg paralysis	Thorough physical exam; blood and urine tests; X-rays; electrocardiogram (EKG), echocardiogram, sonogram	Depending on specific diagnosis: drug treatments, such as beta blockers or calcium channel blockers, a diuretic (for congestive heart failure), blood clot reducers; also, diet, in particular a low-salt diet; even pacemakers

heart rate), lethargy, difficulty breathing, and, possibly, leg paralysis. Diagnosis is reached first through a physical exam, including bloodwork, followed by one or more of the following: chest X-rays, an electrocardiogram, an echocardiogram, or a sonogram. In older cats, hyperthyroidism and hypertension must also be ruled out as an underlying cause.

Yes, Cats Get Heartworm Disease

Usually thought of as a problem affecting dogs, cats, too, can get heartworm. This disease, though it affects the heart, is different from other forms of feline heart disease in that its cause is external: mosquitoes transmit the larvae of the heartworm parasite to your cat. Once the larvae penetrate your cat's skin and invade the tissues, they continue to grow bigger as they migrate; after they take up lodging in your cat's heart, these worms can grow as long as fourteen inches. Left untreated, they can cause death.

Cats with heartworm may show little or no change for several months, until the worms have grown significantly, at which point cats typically become weak and have trouble breathing. Note, however, that a cat may have heartworms but not heartworm disease. A cat's heart can usually tolerate a few adult worms for many months, until the number of worms increases and/or they increase markedly in size.

If you consider your cat to be at high risk for heartworm disease (she goes outdoors and is exposed to mosquitoes), consult your vet about the best way to proceed with prevention and treatment, should it become necessary.

Hyperthyroidism

Hyperthyroidism, the most common hormone imbalance found in older cats (especially cats over ten), is caused by an overactive thyroid producing too much thyroid hormone. Hyperthyroidism is

AT A GLANCE: HYPERTHYROIDISM

Symptoms	Diagnosis	Treatment(s)
Weight loss; hyperactivity; excessive drinking and urination; abnormal vocalizing; intolerance to heat; vomiting or diarrhea; hair loss or "ratty" coat	Blood test (called a T4) to measure the level of thyroxine; if inconclusive, other tests such as the Free T-4 may be run	Most commonly, either antithyroid drugs, surgical removal of the thyroid, or radioactive iodine treatment; for milder forms, alternative treatments may be viable

generally caused either by an enlarged thyroid gland or the presence of a benign tumor in the thyroid gland, and left untreated can lead to heart or kidney failure and, eventually, death.

If your geriatric cat shows any of the symptoms of hyperthyroidism—such as weight loss, need to drink more and urinate more often, "speeded-up" metabolism, excessive vocalizing, and intolerance to heat—waste no time in taking her to your vet for the necessary blood tests used to diagnose this dangerous disease.

(Note: Hypothyroidism, when the thyroid fails to produce enough thyroid hormone, is common in dogs but rare in cats.)

Kidney Disease (Chronic Renal Failure)

Kidney disease is one of the leading causes of death in older cats. As a cat ages, her kidneys may begin to function less efficiently, failing to filter the waste products and toxins from the blood and into the bladder, for release in urine. Instead, these toxins circulate to the kidneys and build up in the blood. If not diagnosed early and treated, the body as a whole begins to break down, leading eventually to death.

Elderly cats are especially prone to the chronic form of kidney disease called chronic renal failure (CRF), marked by gradual (over months or even years) and irreversible loss of kidney function.

AT A GLANCE: KIDNEY DISEASE

Symptoms	Diagnosis	Treatment(s)
Loss of appetite and accompanying weight loss; increased thirst and excessive urination; difficulty urinating; failure to use litter pan or "missing" the pan; lethargy or weakness; unkempt coat	Blood and urine tests; possibly X-rays or ultrasound of the kidneys	Subcutaneous (under the skin) hydration; low-protein diet; possibly medication, to treat related problems such as hypertension; possibly an appetite stimulant; rarely, kidney transplant (very expensive and not usually an option for elderly cats)

Though there is no cure for chronic kidney disease, it can be managed, long term in some cases (see Tommy's story), depending on its stage at the time of diagnosis. Unfortunately, sometimes as much as two-thirds of kidney function may be lost before the disease is caught, making early diagnosis key. To that end, vets often begin to test for kidney failure as part of the senior cat wellness exam. If your cat is losing weight and drinking dramatically increased quantities of water, in conjunction with increased urination, take her in to see your vet as soon as possible.

Liver Disease

As one of the largest glands in the body of a cat, and serving many complex functions, the liver is subject to damage from a number of disorders. As individual cells in the liver become damaged by disease, the organ's ability to function decreases. If the disease is left unchecked, liver failure may result. But, miraculously, the liver can regenerate; so if caught early enough and treated properly, a cat diagnosed with liver disease can recover or be treated long term. The keyword is "early," though, because often by the time you notice a problem, the liver may be as much as 70 to 80 percent damaged.

AT A GLANCE: LIVER DISEASE

Symptoms	Diagnosis	Treatment(s)
Loss of appetite and weight; listlessness; jaundice (yellowing of skin, gums, and whites of eyes); increased thirst; dark yellow urine; fluid buildup in the abdomen	Palpation of abdomen; exam of eyes and gums for jaundice; bloodwork; possibly a liver biopsy	Varies based on specific type of disease: may require appetite stimulation or nutritional/dietary changes; supplements such as milk thistle; drug therapy, typically containing antibiotics, steroids, and immunosuppressives

In older cats, the signs of liver disease—which may appear quickly or slowly—include loss of appetite, followed by weight loss, listlessness, jaundice, increased thirst, dark urine, fluid buildup in the abdomen (which you may mistake as the onset of obesity), and pale or yellow gums.

Five types of liver disease affect cats:

- Hepatic lipidosis (fatty liver disease), which is usually a reaction to another problem, is commonly seen among overweight cats and is potentially fatal.
- Toxic injury is caused by poisoning, bacterial toxins, or lack of blood to the liver.
- Infection or inflammation of the bile ducts and/or liver is usually seen in conjunction with an infectious disease such as feline infectious peritonitis (FIP) or feline leukemia (FeLV).
- Liver cancer, which, though rare in cats, may occur when another form of the disease spreads to the liver.
- Abnormal communication between blood vessels, causing blood to bypass the liver, called portosystemic shunts, is usually a congenital condition.

Other Common Concerns

Other common health concerns of cats include:

- *Feline lower urinary tract disease (FLUTD).* Signs of this disease common to cats include frequent attempts to urinate, straining while doing so, and small amounts of urine passed. Other signs are obsessive licking of the genital area, urinating outside the box, and a preference for cool, smooth surfaces such as the bathtub or a tile floor. FLUTD has a variety of causes: urinary tract infections (UTIs), urinary stones, urethral plugs, cancer, and others. Treatment will depend on the cause, though dietary recommendations are almost always part of the regimen.
- *Hypertension.* More commonly known as high blood pressure, in older cats it is primarily caused by chronic kidney disease, though there may be other causes as well. As in humans, hypertension in cats is very dangerous in that it causes injury to major organs—the heart, kidneys, blood vessels, brain, and eyes. Note that an estimated 60 percent of cats with chronic renal failure (CRF) also have hypertension.
- *Incontinence.* The inability to control urination or defecation voluntarily is not a disease, but it is linked to many aging-cat illnesses and conditions. Among the many health problems that may contribute to incontinence are: kidney disease (chronic renal failure), diabetes, and urinary tract infections. If your cat is taking certain drugs, she may drink more water and need to urinate more often. Or if your cat has arthritis or mobility problems, it may be difficult for her to get in and out of the litter pan. Onset of cognitive dysfunction syndrome (CDS), may also be a contributing factor.

  For owners, incontinence is one of the most difficult aspects of caring for an aging cat. In addition to the obvious problem of cleanup, many struggle with feelings of anger and impatience, sometimes followed in quick succession by guilt for scolding the cat. Depending on the cause of incontinence in your cat, in some cases it can be alleviated, for example, by adjusting medication levels (only your vet should do this). In other cases, it will require adjustments on your part—for example, by supplying your cat with a new "low-rise" litter pan, and perhaps setting out more than one pan, near her favorite places.

- *Inflammatory bowel disease (IBD).* IBD is not one disease, but a group of gastrointestinal disorders, to which older cats are susceptible (though cats of any age may get IBD). The most common signs are chronic bouts of vomiting and diarrhea. Diagnosis typically begins with complete blood count and other tests, primarily to rule out other causes, but ultimate diagnosis is via examination of a tissue sample obtained by surgery or endoscopic exam. Treatment is a combination of dietary and drug therapies.
- *Upper respiratory infections (URIs).* "Cat colds" are not, in and of themselves, serious, but they can cause secondary infections that may lead to chronic problems. Therefore, if your cat has a runny nose, is coughing and/or sneezing, and is having trouble breathing, take her to the vet sooner rather than later. (Also, refer to the sidebar in Chapter 4, which identifies more serious and highly contagious infectious diseases in cats.)

SUMMARY

It's inevitable: your lap warmer will get sick one day. You know that, but somehow it never makes the bad news easier to accept when it comes. And before you even have a chance to deal with your own feelings, you must begin to cope with the practicalities. Your vet will explain what's wrong with your cat, of course, and give detailed treatment and care options and requirements. But it will be up to you to decide how you will proceed, to consider how much you can handle practically and financially, and to determine what is best for your cat. The more you know in advance, the better you'll understand what you are facing when the time comes, and the better equipped you'll be to make informed decisions, so that you can chart the right course for you and your cat.

KEY PET POINTS

- Make sure you thoroughly understand your cat's diagnosis, prognosis, and treatment options. It's a good idea to ask your vet to write down this information, so that you can review it carefully at home and have it on hand should you decide to consult a specialist.
- Many types of treatments, both traditional and alternative, are now available for many age-related feline conditions. Keep your mind open to the possibilities.
- Be honest with yourself and with your vet when it comes to designing a treatment plan for your cat. If you are squeamish when it comes to handling needles, for example, or cleaning wounds, be up front about it so that both you and your cat can get the help you need.

CHAPTER 7

Dollar Signs: Managing the Costs of Senior Pet Care

Finance managers often conduct cost-benefit analyses to determine whether the benefit of doing something is worth the money it takes to do it. No such cut-and-dry method exists for evaluating the benefits versus the costs of caring for your aging cat. After all, you can't put a price tag on keeping your best friend alive and well and by your side for as long as possible. Still, money is a concern for many pet owners. All the advances made in veterinary medicine in the recent past come at a price, some of them at a very high price—into the many thousands of dollars, in some cases. And that's not counting the cost of premium food, mobility aids, and whatever other supplies may be necessary to keep your cat comfortable and safe in his golden years. In the last five years, costs for veterinary services have risen 73 percent, to $19 billion; and according to the American Pet Products Manufacturers Association (APPMA), Americans spent $36.3 billion on pet care in 2005.

Even though most pet owners report they would do anything it takes to save their pets, that "anything" can translate into financial hardship. In worst-case scenarios, people may feel forced to give up their cats (one of the main reasons given for turning pets in to shelters is cost of care); others who can't afford expensive medical care will have their cats euthanized instead. How can you avoid going to such extremes?

You already know four of the best ways to keep the cost of care down for your aging cat:

1. Take your cat for biannual (twice-yearly) checkups.
2. Feed your cat high-quality food.
3. Control your cat's weight.
4. Exercise and groom (including dental care) your cat regularly.

Together, these preventive measures are worth more than a pound of cure; they can add up to a ton of savings. In particular, when you take your cat in for regular checkups, your vet can detect internal disease processes before (sometimes long before) they exhibit external signs. As in human medicine, the earlier problems are detected and treated (or, ideally, prevented), the less expensive they will be over the long term.

THE STORY OF BUSTER: A WEIGHTY ISSUE

Buster is part of a brother-and-sister act, and he's clearly the Jerry Lewis to his sister Mia's Dean Martin. Barely a handful together when they were adopted by Susan from a "garage menagerie" at six weeks old, they were soon taking their act on the road, moving to beautiful Marin County, California, where their "manager" was to begin work at a new job. The soft, gray kittens took the edge off the discomfort that big changes always bring.

Spayed and neutered at six months old, both cats began to grow—and grow. Buster, in particular, seemed destined to be a Big Boy and, unfortunately, to have a weight problem. Susan was careful never to overfeed them—keeping them strictly on a dry food recommended by the cats' vet, in proper amounts. By about age four, Buster's waistline had expanded markedly. (Mia, petite of head, limbs, and paws, too began to put on some belly fat, but nothing like that of her brother.)

Still, the cats thrived. The only health issue was Mia's minor eye condition, which she'd had since birth and which was eventually cleared up with a regimen of eye drops. And though their home included front and back-yards and well-tended gardens, the cats were kept indoors for safety, protected from the wildlife that roamed the river running through Susan's property. Though, from time to time, under Susan's watchful eye, they were allowed out to get an up-close-and-personal view (and sniff) of all that they saw through the many windows in the sun-drenched house.

At around age five, Buster developed a solo act as a superhero—Bustie Man. Stretched out in Susan's arms, his polydactyl paws expanded like wings, Buster liked nothing better than to "fly" around, aloft and going in circles, with well-charted dips and turns for added thrills. (Mia seemed to prefer a more subdued artistry. Her expertise was in rolling on her back and exposing her belly—which might just as well have had a sign on it reading RUB ME.)

Then, as it does for all of us, the lack of "real" exercise began to take its toll, especially on Buster, who was now weighing in at eighteen pounds. The toll had to be paid in the cats' ninth year, when, arriving home from a two-week vacation with her boyfriend, Susan was alerted by her cat sitter that she had noticed the water bowl being emptied very quickly, and the litter box unusually wet with cat pee. Since Mia and Buster shared food and water dishes and the litter box, Susan first had to figure out which cat was making the extra trips to both. Within a day or two, convinced it was Buster, she took him to the vet immediately.

Buster was diagnosed with Type I diabetes. Given the choice between administering insulin pills or injections, Susan, "scared to death at the prospect of giving Buster shots," initially opted for the pills. But as it is with so many cats, pilling became a "nightmare," so back Susan went to the vet for training in administering the shots. Using a plum as a surrogate, Susan quickly became adept at giving Buster the injections twice a day.

At the beginning of Buster's treatments, the vet tested various types of insulin for the best response (requiring frequent and expensive visits until Buster was stabilized), and recommended a low-carbohydrate diet. (But in spite of acknowledging Buster's weight problem, the vet, says Susan, only vaguely mentioned that it would be good if Buster got more exercise.) At the same time, Susan began to read a good deal about Buster's condition, so that "she could better understand what the insulin does and how and why it should be administered." She wanted to find out the "why behind the what."

Buster (top) and Mia: Intermission

The "how" has become a challenge, too, for a number of reasons. Buster has to be fed on a strict schedule, to ensure that he gets his insulin with food, approximately every twelve hours. And Buster, true to his species, sees no reason why he should eat according to the clock, and so Susan must watch him carefully to "make sure things happen as close to on-schedule as possible." Organizing "cat patrol" when she's away has also become more difficult: "Not every pet sitter is willing and/or able to give Buster his shots, and fewer are willing to deal with the inconvenience of coming back over and over if he's feeling finicky and doesn't eat on schedule," says Susan. Finally, Susan has been struggling to start her own business since Buster was diagnosed, and without a steady income, the cost of cat care has become, she says, "a sensitive issue." The insulin costs are high, as is the price of special cat food, along with the requisite regular checkups at the vet. But whether or not she will continue with Buster's treatment has never been in question. Susan says, "I'd rather take in a lodger than sacrifice his medicine."

One aspect of his care has become easier, however. Within about six months of Buster's diagnosis, Susan's veterinary practice changed ownership, and Buster and Susan are currently being helped by a doctor "who is more involved, more empathetic, and tries to educate rather than dictate," an approach and attitude Susan says she really appreciates. It is now two-plus years since Buster was diagnosed with diabetes and, Susan says, "he's as fat and happy as he ever was"—though she recognizes the "fat" part is not a good thing and is making an effort to get Buster "into the gym" more often.

Buyer Beware

The costs of your cat's veterinary care should be commensurate with the degree and depth of specialized care he is receiving. Never let price be your only criterion, or you may get what you pay for. For example, a clinic offering a low-cost spay/neuter operation may not administer IV fluids after surgery, provide post-op pain relief, or even use sterile surgery techniques. When you comparison shop, ask more than how much; ask for the details of procedures and policies as well.

Eventually, most owners of aging cats will find themselves staring down at a bottom line with way too many digits. As you know by now, senior cats—and especially those into their geriatric years—are much more likely to require high-price surgeries, daily meds, and other therapies. In fact, two-thirds of your cat's health problems will occur in the last one-third of his life. It will be tough enough coping practically and emotionally with the fading health of your purr-ball; why not take steps to minimize the worry about whether you'll be able to afford his care? Here are some guidelines for taking the bite out of the costs of caring for your senior cat:

- Think ahead.
- Take advantage of cost-saving programs.
- Avail yourself of other cost-cutting options.

THINK AHEAD

The best way to ensure you'll be able to cover the cost of your pet's care over the long term is to think about it well before you have to pull out your wallet.

Do Some Research

It will help to have some idea what veterinary costs might be over the life of your cat. This kind of information is readily available. Here are some places to start:

- Take a quick trip to the Web site of the American Society for the Prevention of Cruelty to Animals (ASPCA), www.aspca.org, where you can find estimated pet costs. At the home page, click on "Pet Care," search on "Pet Care Costs," then launch the Flash player and choose "Cat" (if you can't run the Flash player, click on the download option). There you'll find a neatly laid-out table of costs, divided into annual, capital, and special sections.
- If you have a purebred cat, you might also want to familiarize yourself with his breed's susceptibility to certain health disorders, which can help prepare you for possible veterinary costs down the road. A good place to do that is the online version of the *Merck Veterinary Manual*, which you'll find at www.merckvet manual.com/mvm/index.jsp. There you can search, for free, by topic, species, specialty, disease, and keyword.

Save for a Rainy Day

It's a familiar refrain, but one of the most effective ways of preparing yourself for the long-term care of your cat is to open a savings account for him—put money aside each month, for example, as you would for a child's education, so that the money will be there when you need it. This is a common recommendation among financial planners for their pet-owner clients.

Buy Health Insurance for Your Cat

Pet insurance has been around for a while now, but, currently, only a very small percentage of pet owners invest in it—around 5 percent (for 3 percent of dogs and 1 percent of cats) according to the APPMA's National Pet Owner's Survey, although this is up from just 1 percent approximately a decade ago. As more pet owners take advantage of the increasingly specialized services offered by the veterinary community, with their higher costs, pet insurance is likely to become an integral part of veterinary medicine.

The considerations for selecting pet insurance are much the same as for human health insurance: price of premiums, deductibles, exclusions for preexisting conditions, and so on. And, needless to say, older cats are considered higher risks, so you'll pay more for coverage—if you can get it at all. Therefore, investing in pet health insurance is best done before your cat is older and needs it. That said, if your senior cat is healthy, health insurance may still be worth investigating.

Here are three companies offering pet insurance:

Veterinary Pet Insurance (the oldest and best known)
Phone: 800-899-4VPI
Web site: www.petinsurance.com

PetCare Pet Insurance
Phone: 866-275-PETS
Web site: www.petcarepals.com

Petshealth Care Plan
Phone: 800-807-6724
Web site: www.petshealthplan.com

Be diligent in your investigation of any pet insurance provider:

- Read the policies thoroughly, including the fine print, especially as it applies to older pets and preexisting conditions, premiums, co-pays, and annual caps.
- Call your state's insurance department to make sure any company you're considering doing business with is registered with state regulators. Not all companies are approved in all fifty states.
- If you go online to check out these companies, verify that all your questions are answered. If you're not sure, call and request paper copies of the policies.
- Sit down with your calculator to figure out what these policies will cost over the predicted lifespan of your cat. Then, as accurately as possible, calculate what you've already been spending out-of-pocket on pet care each year. Compare the numbers. Also consider potential "catastrophic" expenses: Would you be able and/or willing to pay, for example, $6,000 to $10,000 if your cat became seriously ill near the end of his life expectancy? And be aware that, to date, most policies require you to pay for your vet's services at time of treatment; you then file a claim and wait for approval and reimbursement. However, HMO-type programs are becoming more widely available. With this type of policy, you don't pay up front; your vet submits the paperwork to the insurance company to get paid.

The AVMA, which supports the concept of pet health insurance, has identified a number of criteria that any pet health insurance program should meet. It should:

1. Have the support of the veterinary community (veterinary associations, private practitioners).
2. Allow pet owners to choose their own veterinarian and to seek referrals of their choosing.

3. Comply with the policies of the insurance commission of the state in which the policies are issued.
4. Give clear control to the veterinarian to monitor the health of the pet.

TAKE ADVANTAGE OF PROGRAMS

Unlike pet health insurance, which puts senior cats at a disadvantage because of their age, you may be able to get some bottom-line relief in the form of cost-saving programs that actually put old cats first in line.

Package Programs

To educate pet owners about all-important biannual exams for its "senior citizens," a number of veterinary practices across the country offer cost-saving package care programs for their patients over seven years of age. Rather than charging individually for the standard components of the wellness exam (see Chapter 4), they charge a flat rate for the entire workup, sometimes cutting the cost by as much as a third.

Awareness Programs

During various months in the year, to promote senior pet awareness programs, humane organizations, clinics, and even some private veterinary practices show their support by cutting costs, either for overall care or just for a "featured" health issue. For example:

- Every November, the ASPCA celebrates "Adopt-a-Senior-Pet Month" nationwide; other local humane organizations have followed suit with similar programs (though not always at the same time), and many offer lower-cost senior care coverage to promote awareness.
- As noted in Chapter 5, the American Veterinary Medical Association (AMVA), along with veterinary dental organizations,

celebrates National Pet Dental Health Month, usually in February (see www.petdental.com). Find out where in your community deals may be offered for dental checkups and cleanings (your vet's office may be one of them).

Don't hesitate to nose around for others: ask your vet if he or she participates in any low- or reduced-cost care programs; call your local humane organization or veterinary hospital to find out whether they sponsor low- or reduced-cost clinics for yearly vaccinations; and check with other cat owners you know.

"Angel" Programs

If you are a low-income pet owner, you may be able to find financial assistance in the form of an "angel," an individual or an organization that helps qualified pet owners get their cats the care they need when they can't afford it themselves. All the vets interviewed for this book were aware of such angels in their midst—though understandably, these Good Samaritans do not "advertise," so you'll have to ask for help if you need it. Your vet is the best place to start; or call your local humane organization.

You can also do some research into organizational assistance programs. Humane organizations as well as professional veterinary associations typically sponsor these. Here are three, to give you some idea of the various forms of aid available:

- The Marin Humane Society (Marin County, California) sponsors a SHARE (Special Human-Animal Relationships) program, the largest part of which is its Side-by-Side program. Side-by-

Side matches financial support, volunteer efforts, and donated services with qualified pet guardians in need. Depending on the situation, pet owners may receive pet food, veterinary care, grooming, regular visits by volunteers, transportation to the veterinarian or groomer, and much more. Side-by-Side is currently assisting some 220 pet owners with 196 cats (as well as 150 dogs and 38 birds). 415-883-4621; www.marinhumanesociety.org

- The American Animal Hospital Association (AAHA) launched its Helping Pets Fund in 2004 to help those in need get quality care for sick or injured pets.The AAHA fund offers aid for three types of cases: low-income individuals on government assistance; pet owners experiencing a financial hardship; and Good Samaritans who find an animal in need, whether abandoned or owned by someone who cannot afford to care for it. Note that this fund does not give money directly to individuals; an AAHA-accredited veterinary clinic must apply on behalf of them. 866-4HELPETS; www.aahahelpingpets.org
- Human senior citizens with senior pets may find help through the Pets for the Elderly Foundation (PEF), described in Chapter 4. 866-849-3598; ww.petsfortheelderly.org

Wellness Programs

Another cost-saving option comes in the form of wellness programs, which offer comprehensive, affordable health care services. For the price of enrollment, you can save as much as 50 percent on routine medical care for your pet, and you are typically given the option to pay in advance or in low, monthly payments. Two programs to check out are:

- Banfield Optimum Wellness Plans, offered through nearly four hundred PetSmart superstores across the country. Read more about them at www.petsmart.com/banfield, or call PetSmart at 623-580-6100.

- Pet Assure, a pet care saving program, offers a 25 percent discount every time you visit one of its 2,500 participating vets. (Note: Some companies now offer this program as an employee benefit. Check with your human resources department. If they don't offer it now, they might consider looking into it. Employers can call 888-789-PETS, or e-mail employeebenefits@petassure.com to learn more.) To find a Pet Assure provider in your area, go to www.petassure.com.

AVAIL YOURSELF OF OTHER OPTIONS

Four other options you might want to consider for helping you manage your cat's care costs are:

- *Comparison shop for medications and supplements.* Purchasing medications directly from your vet is almost always much more expensive than if you purchase them from a pet supply catalog, an online pharmacy, a compounding pharmacy (which custom-prepares meds), or even from your own pharmacy. Though you will still need a written or phoned-in prescription from your vet, with this in hand, you can find a number of cost-effective alternative sources for your cat's medications. Here are three places to start:

  Internet Pets: www.internetpets.com
  Drs. Foster & Smith: www.drsfostersmith.com
  Pet Med Express: www.1800petmeds.com

- *Get a second opinion on expensive procedures and treatments.* This is just common sense. You'd do it for yourself or another member of your human family before undergoing major surgery, for example, and it's a good practice where your cat is concerned, too.

Safety First

Though your goal in comparison shopping for medications is to save money, price should *not* be your primary criterion: safety should. Especially if you prefer to shop on the Web, you must take the precaution of checking out any online pharmacy before you buy. Your cat's life may depend on it, as well as your own security. Red flags to watch for: if the pharmacy does not require a prescription from your vet, go elsewhere; if the pharmacy requests personal information from you, such as your Social Security number, back out of there. Due diligence in this regard is easy enough: either call the National Association of Boards of Pharmacy (NABP) at 847-698-6227, or go to its Web site, www.nabp.net, to find out if the pharmacy you're considering doing business with is licensed and in good standing. The best advice is to get a recommendation from someone you know and trust. Generally, even your vet will be happy to steer you to cheaper sources to ensure your cat gets the treatment he needs.

- *Consider credit.* Going into debt is never a good idea, but in dire straits, it may be your only option. If you find yourself in this position and your cat needs treatment *now*, check out CareCredit, a health care payment plan that offers several payment options, one of which is interest-free as long as you can pay at least the minimum monthly payment. Learn more about CareCredit at http://carecredit.com, or call 800-859-9975. You may also be able to work out a payment plan with your veterinarian, especially if you have a longstanding relationship and have always paid your bills on time.
- *Contact your local animal shelter.* They may operate or know of a local subsidized veterinary clinic or assistance program.

SUMMARY

Our cats are worth their weight in gold to us, and we can't imagine anything we wouldn't do for them. But then comes the day we have to imagine exactly that: we have to somehow put an actual dollar figure on our love and care. It's never easy to do, but by taking the shock value out of the equation, you'll have an easier time of it. Remember, two-thirds of your cat's health problems will occur in the last one-third of his life. Enjoy the first two-thirds of your cat's years with you for all they're worth, but prepare yourself for the last third. Money may be a concern, but it doesn't have to be an obstacle to caring for your senior cat. Be proactive; do some research and explore all options.

KEY PET POINTS

- Start today, if you haven't already, implementing the preventive measures discussed throughout this book (biannual exams, proper nutrition, exercise, and grooming). Besides being the most conscientious way to care for your aging cat, these measures are the most effective way to save money on long-term veterinary care.
- If your cat is healthy and still on the young side of old, look into health insurance for him; or open a savings account in his name, so that you'll have the money you need when you need it for major health problems.
- Don't despair if you realize your budget will crack or break under the strain of paying for your cat's just-diagnosed major illness. Help is out there, in the form of programs, financial assistance, and credit plans.

PART 3

Quality-of-Life and End-of-Life Issues

CHAPTER 8

Quality of Life: Answering the Hard Questions

Quality of life is a subjective, personal concept. Though sociologists, economists, and politicians talk about it as a quantifiable measure, usually applying the term to large groups of people for the purpose of defining behavior, establishing economic parameters, or setting public policy, no one can really say what constitutes quality of life for another. Sometimes we even have difficulty expressing for ourselves what it means, especially since it changes over time. So how can we be expected to do that for another species? Nevertheless, that's exactly what we are called upon to do: determine quality of life for our cats as they near the end of their lifespan. As the guardians of our pets' well-being, we must somehow decide for them whether their lives are still worth living.

As close as we are to our cats, as much as we think we understand them, it is at this point that we run up against the familiar communication problem. When our cats become ill, they cannot tell us in so many words what is wrong, where "it hurts"; nor can they tell us whether they still take pleasure in living or that the pain or discomfort they're experiencing is too much to bear.

But we're not flying totally blind here. Just as when they first became ill and gave us signs we learned to recognize, as their disease or illness progresses, cats give quality-of-life clues, too. We need to learn to follow these clues, to ensure that the final days we spend with our cats bring their own kind of joy, borne of respect for a life well lived and for the desire for a peaceful closure to that life. It is by asking, and attempting to answer, quality-of-life questions that those clues reveal themselves:

- What constitutes quality of life for a cat?
- How can I tell when my cat is in pain or discomfort? If so, can my cat's pain be managed, and for how long?
- How much longer does my cat have to live? How will I know when it is time to "let go"?

WHAT CONSTITUTES QUALITY OF LIFE FOR MY CAT?

Cats may not be great communicators when it comes to expressing sickness or discomfort, but it's pretty clear to us when they are content and at peace, which by anyone's definition, are sure signs of quality of life. (Think of your cat basking on a sunny window ledge, rolling over from time to time, as if on an invisible rotisserie, to get all her sides equally warmed.) Conversely, the absence of that contentment is a reliable benchmark that her quality of life is on the wane. Of course, as your cat has aged and become ill or disabled, her displays of pleasure probably have become more subdued and short lived, but they're no less meaningful.

Vets agree on a number of criteria that constitute quality of life for an aging and/or sick cat, which can be presented as a series of questions you can ask to determine it for your own cat:

- Does she look forward to eating?
- Is she responsive when you come home after a long day out, or does she barely open her eyes in acknowledgment of your arrival?

- Does she sleep comfortably? Or does she prowl throughout the night, sometimes or often howling at the top of her lungs?
- Does she still enjoy exercise, even if it's just from a sitting position, to bat around a catnip-filled bird at the end of a wand, or still take an interest in what the birds are up to in the tree outside her favorite window?
- Is she able to urinate/defecate without difficulty? Or is she often incontinent, or strains when she tries to go? Has her litter pan become something she misses more often than she hits?
- Does she seem content, peaceful? Or does she vocalize—meow loudly, yowl—incessantly, and at nothing?
- How about her temperament: Is she still sweet and loving, or has she become irritable—hissing at strangers, or even at you? Has it become clear she has no interest in interacting with you?

Remember the guideline in Chapter 2 on prevention, to trust your instincts. When it comes to sorting through quality-of-life criteria, you must give your instincts and your hunches your full attention. If you "just have a feeling" something's wrong, don't push it aside; follow it up. Your vet can help in this regard, to evaluate the importance of signs from your cat and perceptions from you. He or she has expert knowledge of your cat's health status and, ideally, a great deal of insight into your feelings about the kind and level of care you want and can provide for your cat. That, coupled with your day-to-day experience with your cat will help you answer whether she still has quality of life. Dr. Richard Goldston says, "I usually advise owners that when they see their pet doing virtually none of the things that used to bring them happiness…then at that time I believe we are only prolonging dying, not prolonging meaningful living." Of course, he adds, that assumes your pet is getting proper veterinary care and that there are no other options available to offer a *significant* chance of improvement.

THE STORY OF SYD AND CHAKA: DIARY OF GOOD-BYE

Tuesday, May 3, 2005—Syd didn't eat today, so I'm keeping a watchful vigil. (Just now, as I wrote that, I laughed to think how, when he first began to loudly demand food, literally every time I walked into the kitchen, I became a bit irritated. What I wouldn't give right now to hear him howl or to have him drool all over me as he purrs his heart out.)

Syd has a hyperactive thyroid, so he eats half of a naturally compounded chew twice a day with a high-calorie nutritional supplement added to entice him. This morning, when he wouldn't eat his thyroid chew pill—even with the Nutrical that he loves all over it—I knew all was not right. (I call him the Boney Boy, since he's melting away to nothingness.) And when he wouldn't join his brother and sister for breakfast, concern started to build. Even when, finally, he licked some Nutrical off my finger, there was no energy, and the reality that the end could be today hit solidly home.

Two weeks ago, I looked into his eyes and promised that when I saw pain there it would be the end. Today, there is no evidence of pain or discomfort, but those eyes are void of anything else. He even feels different when I hold him. Just yesterday his heartbeat and energy felt vibrant, but this morning he limply leaned into me, resting his head on my arm. I feel there's an exiting of will—of his essence.

Syd (a shelter rescue), his "brother" Chaka, and I grew up and grew old together (a "sister," Libby, joined us later and completes the family circle). They're all almost nineteen, and have been with me most my adult life, and together they have presented me with age-related ailments and annoyances, none of which seem so perturbing today. They have been such a joy.

Chaka was handpicked from a litter at two weeks old, and he has known nothing but protective love, and has shined that back. But then came old age, and, unfortunately, he has not aged gracefully. He's become a grumpy, demanding old man who screams when he wants attention or simply to announce that he has arrived at his new destination. Mostly it's to tell me that he desires my presence. It has gotten so bad that he wakes me several times during a night, and now it has been weeks since I've had a complete night's rest. (The Siamese in him makes my neighbors think that the loud noise is a baby.) Nothing works to quiet him.

Syd: Green-grass days

Dr. Josie—my holistic, does-house-calls, godsend of a vet—is impressed by their condition, given their age. But, since I worry about preserving the quality of life for both the cats—and me—I pay very close attention to the progression of aging on pretty much a daily basis.

Wednesday, May 4, 2005—Not only is Syd still with me but he is back. Yesterday, after doing an hour of work that needed to get done, followed by some research on aging cats, I went to lie down with him. The research had reinforced my suspicion that he was "going," by explaining that cats often know when the end has arrived and that a forty-eight-hour prior-to-death shutdown of the digestive system is a marker in the process.

After almost an hour of being with him, Syd purred for the first time—softly, but his heart was obviously there and into it. I kept it up by gently talking to and petting him. Around noon, I got out a can of his favorite flavor food and he nibbled just a bit. All day I carried him to and from the water bowl so that he would not get dehydrated.

By evening, I could tell he was feeling better when he sniffed with obvious interest at my bratwurst (that's my boy!). The interest extended to his food, and this morning he was purring and drooling all over me in bed. When I lifted him, his head was held high and the energy was fully back, giving strength to his frail body. And he joyously howled up his usual storm as I went about the preparation of feeding all the cats.

Syd was the last to leave the plate after licking it clean. He returned to his normal space, rather than lying under the table as he had done the day before. And he's already been begging for another serving even though it is only 9:15 a.m.

So...I'm not sure what happened. Maybe he had a twenty-four-hour bug. Maybe when I was gone all day Monday he had decided it was okay to "give up," but then having me around changed his mind. Or maybe I just read too much into his not eating. Scratch that. His not eating *is* significant.

Chaka: Cat in a hat

Whatever the reason, I've got my baby back for however long that means.

This is one of the most painful realities that we go through with our aging cats. One time I thought that Chaka was on his way out of the household. A cyst on his neck popped and, despite twice-a-day cleaning and dressing, he developed an infection. A low-level infection from his bad teeth and gums helped this new infection along, as it moved to vulnerable parts of his body. The poor boy could hardly walk until the antibiotics kicked in. But even Dr. Josie was surprised by how strongly he came back.

Debra Severson, Miami Beach, Florida

(Syd and Chaka's story continues in Chapter 9.)

IS MY CAT IN PAIN?

For many pet owners, this is the first question they want answered when they learn their cat is ill—no one can stand the thought of a loved one suffering. For a long time, scientists debated whether animals *could* feel pain. Seems ridiculous, in retrospect, especially since it is now recognized that humans and animals experience pain in much the same way (our nervous systems are very similar). But there's still controversy over how animals actually experience physical pain and demonstrate it, and thus how we can recognize it. No one questions, however, that pain is an important quality-of-life determinant.

For us, as caregivers, we need to address pain in two steps:

1. Identify pain.
2. Manage pain.

Identifying Pain

The American Animal Hospital Association (AAHA), in its 2005 "Senior Care Guidelines for Dogs and Cats," says, "Any behavioral change or change in vital signs may be an indication of pain." But that statement must be qualified, for as the AAHA points out, signs of pain may be affected by other factors, such as medications your cat is taking. To help pet owners and veterinarians recognize a cat in pain, Pfizer, Inc.'s Animal Health division has identified "pain behaviors" in five categories (adapted and reprinted here with permission of Pfizer Animal Health, www.pfizerah.com):

Posture

- Tucked limbs
- Arched or hunched head and neck or back
- Tucked abdomen
- Lying flat
- Slumping of body
- Drooping of head

Temperament

- Aggressive
- Biting
- Scratching
- Chewing
- Attacking
- Escaping
- Hiding

Vocalization

- Crying
- Hissing
- Spitting

- Moaning
- Screaming
- Purring

Locomotion

- Reluctance to move
- Carrying one leg
- Lameness
- Unusual gait
- Unable to walk
- Inactive

Other

- Attacks if painful site is touched
- Failure to groom
- Dilated pupils
- No interest in food or play

What about emotional pain? Do cats feel it? Most cat owners and veterinary practitioners would say, absolutely. In fact, humans and cats have identical regions in the brain responsible for emotion. And research has shown that cats demonstrate emotional distress in the form of behaviors such as lack of motivation, separation anxiety, obsessive-compulsive disorder (OCD), unresponsiveness, loss of appetite, and others. Distress of this nature can intensify physical pain.

Managing Pain

Advances in veterinary medicine include a better, more thorough, understanding of how animals feel and demonstrate pain. Pain management is now taught as part of the curriculum at many veterinary schools and as part of continuing education programs. There's even a Companion Animal Pain Management Consortium, formed to

Who's Who in Pet Health Care: International Veterinary Academy of Pain Management (IVAPM)

This multidisciplinary organization "seeks to promote the acquisition and dissemination of knowledge related to the biology and clinical treatment of pain in animals." To that end, IVAPM sponsors forums for communication, provides for continuing education for veterinarians in the area of pain recognition and treatment, and offers a certification process for vets interested in specializing in pain management. Their Web site, www.cvmbs.colostate. edu/ivapm, is worth a visit, at the very least to see the video "Is Your Pet in Pain?"

---

educate veterinary professionals and students alike on how to recognize and treat pain in pets. The result is that, today, numerous drug treatment options are available for relieving pain in animals. Vets treat pain in advance, too—for example, before a major surgery.

Depending on the type of pain, whether *acute* (sudden onset and usually sharp and severe) or *chronic* (of long duration or frequent recurrence), single drugs or drug combinations may be used. Numerous drug types are available, including NSAIDs, opiate derivatives, antidepressants, anticonvulsants, local anesthetics, and numerous others. Drug modalities (methods) expand the possibilities for pain management still further. They include:

- Oral
- Injectable
- Transdermal (absorption through the skin)
- Transmucosal (absorption through a mucus membrane)

Pain management isn't all about drugs, either. The AAHA points out that, in combination with or as an alternative to drugs, relief may also be feasible in the form of:

- Acupuncture
- Physical therapy and massage
- Local and regional anesthesia
- Weight management (when appropriate)
- Environmental modification (bedding changes and access aids such as ramps, steps, and other "comfort" products)

However, pain management is complicated by the fact that the experience of pain is highly individual: the same cause of physical pain can yield a wide variety of responses in different cats. For example, one cat with arthritis in her back leg may limp or give another clear indication of discomfort, whereas another might simply slow down, which an owner might understandably mistake as just a sign of aging. Furthermore, response to treatment can vary widely, as well.

Alleviating your pet's pain is essential not just because you don't want to see her suffer, but because pain can actually impede the healing process and cause other problems. Just the stress alone caused by pain can lower your cat's immune system, for example. For all these reasons, it's important that you and your vet work closely together to monitor both your cat's pain and her response and reactions to any prescribed pain protocol.

Probably the most effective way to monitor your pet's status is to use the log system described in Chapter 6. On a calendar, note each day:

- Medications or other treatment your pet receives, including exact amounts, as well as her responses/reactions
- Food and water intake
- Behavior shifts
- Changes in her urine and stool, or problems relieving herself

And keep in mind that you're part of the pain management process, too. All medicine goes down better when administered with

Go to the Videotape

To help pet owners better understand how animals experience pain, the International Veterinary Academy of Pain Management (IVAPM), at Colorado State University College of Veterinary Medicine, has prepared an insightful video titled "Is Your Pet in Pain?" It's viewable for free online at www.cvmbs.colostate.edu/ivapm.

love and patience. How you address your cat's pain and handle the treatment protocol will affect how well she responds. If you're tense and frightened, she will pick up on it; if you're frustrated and impatient, you'll probably be met with resistance. If, on the other hand, you take your time, to give both of you confidence in what you're doing, you will be able to add these moments of tender loving care to your long list of joyful memories shared with your cat. Don't hesitate to ask for help if you're having difficulty facing your pet's pain, disability, or physical impairment; administering medications; or just coping in general. If, for example, you start to find more of your cat's pills turning up in corners and behind furniture, signaling that she's found a way to outsmart you, return to your vet or veterinary technician for a retraining session; or ask if the medication is available in liquid form, which may be easier for you to administer. Think options and solutions; usually you'll find them.

It's About You, Too

Your cat's care may be causing stress, a financial burden, a disruption to your daily life, or all of these. So you must consider your own state of mind at the same time you concern yourself with your cat's quality of life. The caregiver role is not an easy one, and it's all too easy to get lost in it—you're so busy taking care of the one who is sick that you get lost in the shuffle. And after weeks, months, or even years in that role, you shouldn't be surprised if you're feeling overwhelmed, scared, even angry and frustrated, and just plain stressed out. If you don't address those feelings, you'll do a disservice to both you and your cat, because your state of mind is an integral part of the level of care you're able to provide your cat. Ask yourself how your quality of life has changed, for better and for worse, since your animal began to require extra care:

1. Do you find yourself having conflicting emotions? For example, do you ever feel angry at the extra work it takes to care for your pet. (Perhaps you're living with an incontinent cat.) Do you then feel guilty for being angry? On the other hand, do you also feel great joy and gratitude that you can share this time in your pet's life?
2. Do you feel you're learning valuable "life lessons" from the experience, or just learning how to get by on less sleep?
3. Do you find it easier or more difficult to remember to take care of yourself because you must attend to your pet?
4. Have you changed your lifestyle to accommodate caring for your cat? Are you afraid to stay out too long in the evening, because you're worried about your pet? Has it been a while since you've taken a vacation because you don't trust anyone to take proper care of your beloved cat? When you must go away on business, are you distracted and feel you must check in with your pet sitter regularly, even obsessively?
5. How about finances? Has the cost of your pet's treatment put a strain on your budget and, therefore, on you? Has it figured into your decision to treat or not to treat? Have you felt compelled to "shop around" for vets based on price, and then worry that you might "get what you pay for"?

Quality of *your* life at this time is about achieving balance, and to do that you must be honest with yourself. Nobody said it was going to be easy, and of course you'll have your bad days, but if caring for your sick cat is becoming more of a burden than a labor of love, you need to acknowledge that so that you can better determine how to proceed.

HOW WILL I KNOW WHEN TO LET GO?

Thanks to the tremendous progress in veterinary medicine in the past few decades, our cats are living longer lives of quality, sometimes even in the face of serious disease and illness. Not too long ago, many age-related ailments now being handled routinely could only have been "treated" with euthanasia. But these advances are not without their disadvantages. For one, they make it much more difficult for vets to answer the questions all cat lovers have when confronted with the end of their cat's life: How much longer does my cat have to live? Will I know when it's time to cease treatment?

We are fortunate, indeed, to be able to extend the time we spend with these remarkable creatures. And the more time we have with our cats, the stronger the bond between us grows. But the stronger the bond, the more difficult it becomes to "let go"—or to even think about it. But think about it we must, if we are to spare our cats and ourselves greater distress. If we prepare ourselves for the inevitable end of this beautiful friendship, our reward will be the knowledge that we "did right by our cat," as she deserved, and right by ourselves, as we too deserve.

Think About It

What's the best way to prepare yourself for the loss of your pet? First, just by thinking about it—not pushing those thoughts away when they come. It may help to think of this as an anticipatory grief period. A lot has been written and discussed about the five stages of grief—denial, anger, bargaining, depression, and acceptance—following the death of a loved one, but many of us often go through these stages *before* the loved one dies. In particular, many pet owners are prone to the first stage, denial. As discussed in Chapter 2, a common mistake pet owners make is to not see signs from their cats that something is wrong. Sometimes not seeing is a function of not paying attention; but it might also be a function of *not wanting to see*—you know, denial. We know our cat is at the end of her lifespan; we know she's sick; and we know she won't live forever. But still we may refuse to acknowledge those facts in our "heart of hearts." We hang on, literally, for dear life. You will have to find the way that works best for you to break through the denial.

Talk About It

For many people, it helps to talk to others, those who know us and know our cat, and who understand the importance of this relationship in our lives. Those who have gone through the process themselves are particularly helpful. Your vet may be able to put you in touch with another client who is willing to share his or her letting-go process in an effort to help you through your own.

Another option is to join an online chat group. Because of the digital distance conferred by the technology, this may be an easier venue in which to communicate at this emotional time—you can come and go as you please and participate as much or as little as you wish. Two to check out are: www.pethobbyist.com and www.cathobbyist.com/chat. Or type in search parameters such as "cat chat room" or "pet chat room," and you'll find many more choices.

Consult with Your Vet

It's always a good idea to keep your vet in the loop, not just about your cat's health but your state of mind as well. That is the only way he or she can properly advise you at this difficult time. Your vet can't make your decision for you, but he or she can ease the way for you. You might want to make an appointment with your vet for the express purpose of determining when to cease active treatment, especially if your cat is terminally ill. Ironically, this has been made more difficult by the very science and technology that gave our aging cats quality lives for so long. Many treatment protocols can be continued for extended periods of time, so the question that must be asked is, at what value? At some point, we are, as Dr. Goldston said, prolonging dying, not meaningful living.

You may even want to consider seeking a second opinion at this juncture, because veterinarians, too, become emotionally invested in the care of their patients and sometimes have trouble acknowledging the true circumstances of a situation, and thus want to continue making heroic attempts at cure.

Who's Who in Pet Health Care: American Association of Human-Animal Bond Veterinarians (AAH-ABV)

The threefold mission of the AAH-ABV is to "further veterinary awareness, scientific progress, and educational opportunities in the area of the human-animal bond; to encourage veterinary participation in human-animal bond activities with related organizations and disciplines; and to explore the potential for establishing a veterinary specialty in the area of human-animal bond." For more on this organization in general, and its approach to veterinary hospice specifically, go to http://aahabv.org.

Provide Hospice Care

"When the goal of treatment begins to shift from curing illness to providing comfort, it is time to consider hospice." That's the guideline of the American Association of Human-Animal Bond Veterinarians (AAH-ABV). A logical outgrowth of the modern human hospice movement, which began in the 1970s, veterinary hospice care is fast becoming a widely recommended and implemented end-of-life care program for terminally ill and seriously disabled companion animals.

In its "Senior Care Guidelines for Dogs and Cats," the American Animal Hospital Association (AAHA) cites the American Veterinary Medical Association (AVMA) definition of veterinary hospice care as "giving clients time to make decisions regarding a terminal companion animal and to prepare for [its] pending death, while always taking into consideration the comfort of the animal." The AAH-ABV defines it as a system that "provides compassionate comfort care to patients at the end of their lives and also supports their families in the bereavement process." To that end, it includes "comprehensive nursing care as well as psychosocial and spiritual care for the patient and the family."

Many people unfamiliar with the concept of hospice care, whether human or animal, mistakenly think of hospice as a place, such as a hospital or nursing home. In fact, hospice care is given primarily in the patient's home; and for animals, this is almost always the case. Hospice care (also commonly referred to as *palliative care*) for a companion animal is based on the individual's specific requirements. Depending on your cat's disease or illness and age, according to the AAHA, hospice care for your cat might include:

- Outpatient/home care
- Pain management
- Easy access to food, water, and toilet facilities
- Wound management
- A stable and consistent environment
- Good hygiene and sanitation
- Clean bedding and padding
- Mental stimulation

In addition, nutritional maintenance (balancing a therapeutic diet while maintaining caloric intake) is paramount for a cat receiving hospice care, says the AAHA.

If you are interested in providing hospice care, be aware that it will take some planning; therefore, it should be part of the "think about it" stage described earlier. First, you need to ascertain whether your vet is familiar with the concept and is willing to partner with you in this effort. A veterinarian is essential, for it is he or she who will design a plan for your cat's treatment, one that can be adapted to meet both your and your cat's changing needs. Typically, home visits by your veterinarian or a member of his or her staff are recommended as part of the program, whenever possible. During this time, your vet should also conduct what is essentially a risk-benefit analysis of any medications and treatments still being provided. Again, the goal is to sustain good quality of life, not prolong dying.

You may also have to do some rearranging of your household and your schedule to accommodate the care plan your vet designs; and you may need help from willing friends or a qualified cat sitter, to administer medications or treatment when you cannot. Hospice care is a loving undertaking, but it does require extra work and commitment on your part, and you should not underestimate what's involved.

The objective of hospice care is, ultimately, a peaceful death for your cat, whether by euthanasia or natural causes. As important as meeting the AAHA guidelines for providing that care is focusing throughout this period on giving your cat regular doses of love and attention, while paying close attention to your own needs and emotions at this important time in both your lives.

SUMMARY

This chapter raised a number of questions, questions difficult to answer because they require us to interpret quality of life for our cat coming to the end of that life. At the same time we are trying to do what's best for our cat, we often are consumed with feelings of con-

To Learn More About Hospice Care . . .

Call 707-557-8595 or go to www.pethospice.org, the Web site of the Nikki Hospice Foundation for Pets, the first official organization committed to providing hospice care for terminally ill or dying companion animals. Here you'll find in-depth FAQs about the foundation, as well as hospice care in general, and links related to pet loss.

fusion and conflict. We may seesaw between the urge to ease our cat's passing, when we know she is suffering, and the temptation to do whatever it takes at whatever cost to keep her alive for just a little while longer. It is at this time that we must answer the call to return the unconditional and unselfish love our cats have given us throughout their lives with us: we must let go. In the next chapter, we talk about the most difficult aspect of caring for an aging cat: deciding it is time to euthanize her.

KEY PET POINTS

- Tune in to clues from your cat that her quality of life may be in jeopardy, and follow those clues.
- Familiarize yourself with pain behaviors, just as you learned to recognize signs of illness.
- Work closely with your vet in managing your cat's pain treatments and/or therapies. Continuous monitoring is essential.
- Consult with your vet about the feasibility of providing hospice care for your cat, while preparing yourself for the heart-wrenching effort of letting go.

CHAPTER 9

Farewell, Friend: Coming to Terms with End of Life

It's unclear when the euphemism "put to sleep" came into widespread use as the alternative for euthanizing companion animals. Perhaps it was coined to soothe the breaking hearts of so many pet owners who hope and pray their ailing pets will die peacefully in their sleep. We want this most difficult decision made for us. We want no doubt that the time is right to say good-bye. We may find ourselves looking toward heaven and saying, "Please don't make me do your job for you." But for most of us, this will be our "job," the last we will have to do for our aged and ailing cats. And we will be expected to carry out this final act of care even as we are in the throes of grief. Nothing could be more painful.

MAKING THE DECISION TO EUTHANIZE

There is no way to ease the anguish caused by the impending death of a beloved pet, but by addressing all the issues involved in advance, it is possible to ease the passage, so that the loss is not preceded, and complicated, by feelings of panic, misunderstanding, and uncertainty.

Many people have mixed feelings about euthanasia, and few make the decision easily, and many suffer guilt afterward. You may find yourself thinking such things as, "This goes against nature—I'm killing my cat." But if you consider that all the advanced treatments your cat received—surgeries, medications, and so on—kept him alive longer than nature intended, you may be able to think instead that euthanasia is more a decision to stop artificially keeping your cat alive.

The Good Death

Though some cats do, of course, pass peacefully in their sleep, this is not the norm today. The same advances in veterinary medicine that enable us to keep our cats alive longer, even in the face of serious illness and disease, also force us to make the decision when to stop taking heroic measures—we must acknowledge when we are prolonging dying. Dr. Goldston says that the single gravest misconception pet owners have about their pets is that they will die peacefully, at home, in their sleep. *Euthanasia*, Greek for "good death," is the humane option for most pet owners.

You may also feel you're "giving up," and maybe too soon. Shouldn't you seek another opinion, try another treatment, research other options? The best way to address this feeling is in close consult with your veterinarian. In its "Senior Care Guidelines for Dogs and Cats," the American Animal Hospital Association (AAHA) recommends that vets aid their clients in "assessing their animal's welfare and in making an ethical decision" by considering the "five freedoms," as established by the London-based Farm Animal Welfare Council (FAWC). These are:

- Freedom from hunger and thirst
- Freedom from discomfort
- Freedom from pain, injury, and disease
- Freedom from fear and distress
- Freedom to express normal behavior

For example, critical decision points for you may be when your cat has trouble breathing, no longer eats or drinks enough to sustain himself, cannot get comfortable when he tries to rest or sleep, or shrinks from your touch because he is in pain.

In addition to helping clients evaluate their pet's condition, vets also often ask them in advance about their wishes regarding the euthanasia process and aftercare so that pet owners do not have to make these difficult decisions during a period of emotional duress or crisis (when, say, their cat suddenly and dramatically takes a turn for the worse). If your vet does not request this information from you in advance, you can take the initiative yourself, after considering the following issues:

- Where would you prefer the procedure take place: at home or in the vet's office/veterinary hospital?
- Do you want to be present during and/or after the procedure? Do you want others to attend as well (a friend, family members, children)?
- Do you plan to have your cat's body buried or cremated?

Let's examine each of these issues.

Location

A lot of pet owners want their cat euthanized at home, for a variety of reasons:

- It is less stressful for the cat, especially if he is very ill and/or large and difficult to transport at this stage.
- They want their cat to have all the comforts of home at this difficult time.
- Home ensures privacy for you and anyone else who will be present, and enables you and others to give free rein to your emotions.

But before you choose this option, consider carefully whether having your cat euthanized at home might make the grieving process more difficult for you (and your family) later, because you will be constantly reminded that here is where he died. You should also find out, in advance, whether your vet does home euthanasia. If not, and you're sure this is what you want to do, you can find one who does by logging on to www.athomevet.org, the Web site for the American Association of Housecall Veterinarians (AAHV).

All that said, euthanizing your cat in your vet's office or a hospital need not be cold and impersonal. You can bring your cat's favorite blanket, an article of your own clothing you've worn (your smell will comfort him), or a favorite toy. And vets today go out of their way to make this time as stress-free as possible, typically allowing their clients as much privacy and time before and after the procedure as they need. Vets and their staff know only too well what you are going through and are as compassionate as they are professional, ensuring that your cat has not only the safest treatment, but the kindest as well.

Your Role

Will you be there? Yes! say many pet owners. No matter how difficult, they feel they want to be—must be—there for their cats, to give them comfort and security. It may be a point of honor as well, a desire to pay homage to the unmatched companionship their cats gave to them, to return the favor. For other people, seeing their cat die is simply too traumatic, and they fear they will only upset their cat by being so distraught in his presence. Some ask a surrogate to stand in for them, someone who knows them and/or their cat well and understands why they cannot bear to be in the room at that time. No judgment should be attached to this decision—remember, it's about you, too.

If your cat is the family pet, others in his clan (including other pets) may also want to be present during the euthanasia. If you have decided to have the procedure done at home, this should be no problem. If, on the other hand, it will take place in your vet's office, check in advance whether this is possible. First, some vets do not allow very young children (five years or younger) or other animals to be present during euthanasia; second, too many people crowded into a small treatment room may only add stress to the situation—and to your cat.

Aftercare

You must also think about your cat's body, separate from his spirit, his character. If you do no other planning before your cat dies, decide in advance what you want done with his remains, for you will not want to think about this in the immediate aftermath of his death.

The two major options are burial and cremation, and within each of those choices are two secondary options.

Burial

If you decide you want to bury your cat, how you go about it will depend on where you live. Many people with their own homes choose to situate their cat's grave in their yard—his yard. If this is your inclination, there are two cautions to be aware of:

- First, though your home is your private property, you may be prohibited by local laws from burying your cat there, so be sure to check this in advance. Even if it is allowed, there may be requirements as to the depth of the grave, for health reasons.
- Second, consider how you will feel if you one day move from this residence and must leave your cat's remains behind.

The second burial option is a pet cemetery. These exist now throughout the United States, though you may have to go some distance from your local area to find one. The advantages to this option are that there is no question you will be within the scope of the law; your cat's grave site will be cared for and undisturbed; and you can visit the site as you would any departed family member. Interment at a pet cemetery will cost more, however; and, as with home burial, if you should one day leave the area, you leave your cat behind.

Cremation

Cremation is the preference for many pet owners these days, especially urban dwellers. You can choose group cremation or individual cremation, and you will base your decision on whether you want your cat's ashes returned to you. Cost may also be a consideration, as group cremation is less expensive.

- If you choose group cremation, you generally will be leaving your cat's body with your vet, who will take care of transporting it to a pet crematorium or animal shelter for the process.
- If you choose individual cremation, you will still leave your cat's body with your vet, who will ensure it is handled individually and returned to you—usually in an appropriate box or other container. Once your cat's remains have been returned to you, you may want to put them in a more meaningful or decorative urn and place it appropriately in your home. Or you may want to scatter his ashes, or bury them, in one of his favorite spots.

UNDERSTANDING THE PROCEDURE

When faced with a frightening or upsetting situation, we each handle it in our own way. Some of us find that knowing as much as possible about what will happen calms our fears; for others, the less we know, the better. You know what level of knowledge empowers you and what kind just makes you feel worse, especially when it comes to medical procedures. So it is with the process of euthanasia. You might want to understand exactly what will happen to your

Hallowed Ground

For more information on pet cemeteries, or to find one in your area, check out the International Association of Pet Cemeteries and Crematories site, www.iaopc.com, or go to Moira Allen's Pet Loss Support Web site, www.pet-loss.net. Both also have links to other areas of pet-loss support.

cat, or you may cringe at the mention of any specifics. Therefore, this section only briefly describes the procedure. If you think that a more comprehensive understanding of euthanasia will help give you peace of mind, as part of your advance planning ask your vet to explain in as much detail as you want what your cat will experience.

Most vets today administer a sedative or tranquilizer prior to the euthanasia drug, sometimes in pill form, but more commonly as an injection under the skin, like a vaccination. This calms your cat quickly—and perhaps you, too, just seeing your cat relax. (At this point, you may want a few minutes alone with your cat, to say good-bye.) Next, your vet will insert an intravenous (IV) catheter in one of your cat's veins (often in a back leg). If your vet did not already sedate your cat, he or she may do so now, through the IV catheter and syringe. When you're ready (most vets ask), the vet will administer the euthanasia drug, which is an overdose of a barbiturate. (If you have chosen to have the procedure done at home, the vet may use only a needle and syringe.) Most pet owners who have decided to stay with their cat at this time will gently stroke their cat and speak softly to him.

Very quickly it will be over. Your cat's head may droop or slowly fall over, and your vet will check for a heartbeat to confirm he is gone.

Prepare Yourself

In most cases, dying from euthanasia will seem just like a gentle release of tension, but you should also be aware of the following:

- Your cat's eyes will *not* shut when he dies.
- Your cat's body may twitch, his heart may beat for a couple of seconds after he has stopped breathing, and you may hear sounds, such as sighing.
- There may be a release of your cat's bladder and bowels, so if you plan to hold your cat in your arms or lap while he is euthanized, cover yourself first with a towel or blanket.

Whether at home or at your vet's office, you will probably want to spend a few minutes—or more—with your cat after he has died. Take all the time you need; it is not easy to step away, especially as it will feel you are leaving a big piece of your heart behind.

You will probably not be able to think straight initially, and this is why it is so important to have decided in advance how you will handle your cat's body. If you have decided to cremate your cat, usually your vet will take care of transporting the body to the pet crematorium; if you have decided for a burial in a pet cemetery, in general they will pick up your cat; and if you have decided to bury your cat on your own property, his body will remain with you.

Procedural Variations

Though the procedure described here is typical, each vet will have his or her own euthanasia protocol, depending in part on where you have chosen to have it done.

COPING WITH THE LOSS OF YOUR CAT

Cats break your heart only once, but it's a compound fracture, one slow and painful to heal. Their very absence is a kind of presence. Everywhere they were, you look for them, sense them, see them. Out of the corner of your eye, you catch a flash of movement; you turn quickly to look, expecting to see him there, only to realize your eyes were playing tricks on you.

And you never know when it's going to rise up, this groundswell of emotion for your absent friend. You may prepare yourself for it as you walk through the door at night knowing he won't be there to scold you for being so late; or in the morning, as you wait for your coffee to brew, your hands are uncomfortably idle when they should be filling his bowl, so you fuss with some unnecessary chore or other. But even worse, it comes when you least expect it. You walk into a meeting with a new client, in full professional garb, with attitude to match, sure of yourself and your presentation. Then, suddenly, you see on the client's desk, a picture of him with his children and their cat—a cat not really like yours at all, yet your eyes fill, threatening to spill over. Or you're watching a movie on TV that has nothing to do with cats, or even animals, but it's about loss, and suddenly you're in a puddle of tears.

Grief is like that: it's sneaky and erratic, coming and going, and coming back again. It has no time frame; it keeps no schedule. There is little you can do except "go with the flow," and accept that whatever you are feeling, whenever, wherever, it's the way it has to be for you. What it doesn't have to be is lonely. No matter what your circumstance or living situation, you do not have to grieve alone—unless, of course, that's the way you choose, the way that's best for you. But most people, at least at some point during the grief process, feel the need to talk, to share, to just *be*, with someone else.

THE STORY OF SYD AND CHAKA: DIARY OF GOOD-BYE (continued)

Tuesday, May 10, 2005—We had a scare with Chaka today. As the cats did their normal "greet me in the bathroom" routine after I got out of bed, I noticed bright red drops of blood all over the white tile floor. They came from Chaka—a trail followed him from the living room.

Knowing that once again one of his growths had erupted, I grabbed the needed supplies and locked us in the bathroom to quickly cleanse and dress him. But it was hard. The sore was pouring forth so strongly I almost lost my stomach. I wasn't the only one. Chaka proceeded to vomit and poop in front of me, first on the tile floor and then again in the living room.

I called Dr. Josie, who arrived quickly with her assistant. They cleaned up Chaka some more, shaving his neck and doing a thorough job with hydrogen peroxide. As the sore became more visible with the cleaning, they explained that this time tissue had come out, and that the wound might never completely close back up. I learned how the centers of growths can die, which leaves them susceptible to pus building up and exploding, as it has with Chaka, now three times. I was to continue with my dressing and putting on the little protective sock hat I'd made, which they thought quite nice.

Most important, they confirmed that he was not in any discomfort. Only I am.

Tuesday, May 24, 2005—I knew the end would be today when I first woke. I had gotten up around 5:30 to go to the bathroom. As I often do then, I grabbed the cats who weren't already in bed so that we could spend some time bonding. Syd was uncharacteristically sleeping in the foyer and, when I put him in bed on his pillow, for the first time, he lost control of his bladder.

After cleaning up the linens and mattress, I laid back down with Syd and noted how limp, docile, and weak he was. I was not surprised this time when he did not want to eat. When he started getting wobbly as he walked, and took to hiding, no question remained.

It was the most loving, peaceful, painless end possible. And I was with Syd through it. Well, almost, as he wouldn't—or couldn't—leave with me by his side.

A friend had spent forty minutes with us, and was there for the seizures, which were mild. Thank goodness I had connected with Dr. Josie earlier so I knew what to expect.

A couple of times we thought he had passed and said our good-byes, only to have a small movement tell us we were wrong, which brought some needed levity.

As I sat and stroked Syd, I talked of our wonderful life and told him I was ready to release him. But it wasn't until I walked my girlfriend to the door that he actually left me. So, it was unconditional, adoring love he gave me until the very end.

I'm okay. Really I am. I had asked that my babies go peacefully, with me by their side, and I was blessed to have this prayer answered with Syd. And he was blessed to have me there. I am a bit numb and sad, but it is what it is, and I wouldn't change a thing. Well that's not true—I'd take another few years.

Syd would have turned nineteen in three months. Chaka turns nineteen this weekend.

Friday, May 27, 2005—Syd's passing was easy. His absence is not.

Gone are the days when people felt they had to keep the loss of a beloved pet to themselves, for fear of hearing such remarks as, "It's only a cat; if you feel that bad, just get another one." Though such insensitivity still exists—and there will be times and situations you won't feel comfortable mentioning your loss and grief—in general, the human-animal bond is recognized as one of the most intense and important to people, and its severing by the death of a pet is a well-understood cause of grief and depression.

You've no doubt heard the experience of grief described as a process, defined by Elisabeth Kubler-Ross in her now-classic book, *On Death and Dying* (first published in 1975), as occurring in five stages: denial, anger, bargaining, depression, and acceptance. But this is not necessarily a neat, sequential process, progressing from stage one to stage five, and then you're done and ready to move on. Rather, it can be quite messy and long lasting, and so very disturbing and disruptive. You may zig and zag between the stages, one

Helping Children Cope with Pet Loss

Part of your own grieving process may be to help other members of your family, especially young children, face the death of the family pet.

When a dearly loved cat dies, it is often a young child's first experience with death, and so must be addressed carefully. The child's age and level of maturity, as well as his or her state of mind, must be considered, but generally "honesty is the best policy," as is a straightforward approach. Children are remarkably astute and often can sense what's *not* being said. They're also very literal, so phrases like "putting the cat to sleep" may just confuse a child who may later wonder why the cat can't just "wake up."

It often helps children to understand the finality of death by memorializing their cat in some way—putting flowers on a grave, or planting a tree or bush in the cat's name, for example. They should also be encouraged to express their feelings through drawing, writing, and, of course, talking. Another very effective way to broach the subject is through reading. Three titles worth reviewing for appropriateness to your child or children are: *When a Pet Dies,* by Fred Rogers (Penguin Books for Young Readers, 1998); *Sad Isn't Bad: A Good-Grief Guidebook for Kids Dealing with Loss,* by Michaelene Mundy; illustrated by Robert W. Alley (Abbey Press, 1998); and *I'll Always Love You,* by Hans Wilhelm (Crown Books for Young Readers, 1985).

Keep a close eye on your children at this time, watching for signs of extreme or prolonged distress—loss of appetite, depression, anger, sleeping problems, and so on. In this case, you may need to find professional help.

day angry at your cat for leaving you, or at your vet because there was nothing else she could do; the next day, you wake relieved that your cat is no longer suffering and that you are no longer stressed from the worry and the effort of caring for him, and you accept that you did all that you could; three days later, you're sunk so deeply in sadness you can't see your way out. And so it goes. And go it eventually does. Until then, you may need a helping hand—or heart—to see you through.

Fortunately, today pet-loss grief counseling is widely available. And this is no one-size-fits-all support; it is as highly individualized as the grief process itself. You can join a group, get one-on-one counseling, talk on the phone, connect online, or any combination, to suit your personality, your schedule, and your emotional state. In short, help is there—everywhere—when and where you need it.

Pet-Loss Hotlines

Pet-loss hotlines are call-in programs, staffed by volunteers or professionals or, in the case of veterinary school hotlines, by students. Most of the lines have limited operating hours, usually in the evenings between 5 or 6 and 9 or 10 p.m. Some of the best known are given here, but this list is far from comprehensive. Note that some of these numbers are main switchboards, so you may need to ask to be connected to the pet bereavement hotline. And note that most of the phone numbers will mean a long-distance charge if you're out of the area, so it will be worth your while to call your local humane organization for a hotline in your community; or go to www.aplb.org, the Web site of the Association for Pet Loss and Bereavement (APLB).

University of California-Davis Pet Loss Support Hotline:
800-565-1526 or 530-752-3602
Tufts University, Cummings School of Veterinary Medicine:
508-839-5302

Cornell University Pet Loss Support Hotline: 607-253-3932
Chicago Veterinary Medical Association: 630-325-1600
Colorado State University Veterinary Teaching Hospital/Argus Institute: 970-297-1242

Before the Fact

You don't have to wait until your cat has died to seek help coping. If you're having a difficult time making the decision to euthanize or facing your cat's impending death, connect with someone beforehand to get the support you need.

Online Chat Rooms

As noted in Chapter 8, an increasingly popular venue for talking about pet loss, and finding and giving support, is online. Any time of the day or night, you can log on and find a kindred spirit. Just type "pet loss chat" into your search engine and you'll find hundreds of choices. It's a good idea to spend some time reading through a few of these before you begin to participate, however, to ensure that you find a group you're comfortable interacting with.

Grief Counseling

For many of us, there's just no substitute for personal, face-to-face interaction, especially when we're having a hard time coping with loss. Grief counselors (generally, psychologists or social workers), some specializing in pet loss, will meet with you one-on-one or give you the opportunity to join group sessions as well (you may want to do both). Most humane organizations, shelters, and some veterinary hospitals and clinics also sponsor support groups.

The best way to find a grief counselor or support group is through a personal recommendation. Your vet surely will be able to supply you with one or more names; ask friends, family, and other cat owners, as well. For a state guide to pet support groups and counselors, check out Moira Anderson Allen's excellent Pet Loss Support Web site, www.pet-loss.com.

Animals Know Loss, Too

If yours is a multipet household, be aware that other cats or dogs may feel the loss of the missing cat, too, especially if they were closely bonded. The sudden occurrence of behavior problems following the death of your cat is the typical sign—howling, loss of appetite, lethargy. In most cases, just spending time with your other pets and adhering to their normal routine will comfort and settle them in short order.

Self-Care

During the grieving process, probably no form of support is more important than the support you give yourself. Take time off if you need it. If you think—or know—your employer won't accommodate a pet bereavement period, consider calling in sick—you are, after all, sick at heart. Then take care of yourself. Get plenty of rest and eat right. Exercise, too; it will help you sleep.

Keep good company, with people who will understand what you're going through. Stay away from anyone from the "it's just a cat" school of thought. Or, if you prefer, spend quality time with yourself: go to the movies, read, rearrange the furniture—do whatever it takes to soothe your aching heart.

Finally, take heart. The day will come when you begin to notice that when you think about your absent friend, you're smiling instead of crying. The healing has begun.

SUMMARY

The death of a loved one is a wound, for which there is no salve or bandage except time. But never does time creep so slowly as when we wait for it to apply its healing hands. To help pass this time, we may seek the comfort and compassion of those who understand our bereavement; but in the end, we each must simply live through it.

KEY PET POINTS

- As much as you might wish it otherwise, recognize that you will probably have to decide to euthanize your cat so that he doesn't suffer unnecessarily. And that will be the last, best gift you can give him.
- Learn from your vet what to expect as your cat's disease or illness progresses, to help you decide when to cease treatment. Your vet cannot and will not decide for you, but he or she will give you guidance.
- So that you do not suffer unnecessarily, consider in advance the details of the euthanasia procedure and aftercare.
- Grieve, as you must, but know that you are not alone and that help is available to you in many forms and from many sources.

Epilogue

Just before this book went into production, and almost three months to the day after sharing her diary of the experience of saying good-bye to her elderly cat Syd (see Chapters 8 and 9), I received a sad postscript via e-mail from Syd's owner, telling me that Chaka, Syd's longtime companion (they were both nineteen), too, had passed on. And whereas saying good-bye to Syd had been under the best possible circumstances—at home and peaceful—Chaka's passing couldn't have been more different. It was every cat owner's dread: Chaka had taken a sudden turn for the worse the night before Deb was scheduled to leave for Europe on a business trip that could not be postponed. The next morning when Chaka's own vet could not be reached, Deb called another vet she was familiar with, and, as she put it, "had to play God and make the decision that Chaka's end had come."

"Chaka passed in my arms," she said, "looking and feeling so normal that I could have imagined him in a deep sleep." Five hours later, Deb was on a plane to Europe, "knowing that life goes on but wanting it to just slow down a bit—at least for today."

There are no happy endings in the tale of care for the senior cat. But there are, of course, happy memories. Your cat cannot be replaced. But your relationship with him has expanded your capacity to love; and one day sooner or later—perhaps on the first day you find yourself laughing instead of crying when you think of your cat—you may find yourself wanting to share that love and care with another one. Few people who have been the object of a cat's unique brand of affection ever want to live without it again. When this might happen for you, however, is as personal as the grief you experience. There are those pet owners who plan right away to welcome another cat into their homes and hearts—some even begin planning for the new addition to the family before their senior cat dies. This is their way of helping to cope with the impending loss. Others wait weeks, months, even longer. There is no right time—except the right time for you.

The best guideline here, and one that you've read repeatedly in this book, is to trust your instincts. You'll find you "just happen" to be at the mall at a time when the pet superstore there is sponsoring its weekly adoption day for one of the local humane associations. Maybe you'll turn down the street where you know you can see through the window into the local animal shelter's adoption department. You may not even be aware you're looking, or you'll tell yourself you are *just* looking. Then before you know it, a cat picks you out. That's usually the way it happens: we think we pick them, but most often it's the other way around. They know how to trust their instincts, and they never doubt them. Their keen sense of smell includes having a nose for who is right for them. One day it will be you.

And so it was for Deb. About a month after Syd died, in the company of her twelve-year-old niece, she went into a vet's office where they "show" animals from a rescue service. While playing with two kittens in the window, who were due to go to their new home the next day, Deb was told by a staff member that "in the back" were two five-month-old brothers that would be "going back tomorrow and were not likely to get another chance at adoption" (or, as Deb put it, "a nice way to say they would be put to sleep").

Instead, the "twins," now called CC and Shiva, went home with Deb, and she says, "have brought such life back." Particularly touching to her is that they have chosen as their favorite place to sleep the very spot where Deb found Syd lying on his last day. It is warm there again, and in Deb's heart, too.

Resources

General Information

American Association of Feline Practitioners (AAFP): 800-204-3514 or 908-359-9351; www.aafponline.org

Cat Fanciers' Association: 732-528-9797; www.cfainc.org

Cornell University's Feline Health Center (FHC): 800-548-8937; www.vet.cornell.edu/FHC

National Academies: Advisors to the Nation on Science, Engineering, and Medicine: http://national-academies.org/petdoor

BOOKS: GENERAL CARE

The Cornell Book of Cats: A Comprehensive and Authoritative Medical Reference for Every Cat and Kitten (2nd ed.), by the Faculty, Staff, and Associates, Cornell Feline Health Center, Cornell University; Mordecai Siegal, ed. (Villard, 1997)

First Aid and Emergency Care for Dogs and Cats, by Roger W. Gfeller, DVM, and Michael W. Thomas, DVM, with Isaac Mayo (Pet Care Books, 1994; revised 2004) *Note: This book is available for browsing at www.veterinarypartner.com.*

The Humane Society of the United States Complete Guide to Cat Care, by Wendy Christensen (St. Martin's Press, 2002)

The Pill Book Guide to Medication for Your Dog and Cat, by Kate Roby and Lenny Southam (Bantam, 1998)

WEB SITES

Merck Veterinary Manual: www.merckvetmanual.com/mvm/index.jsp

VeterinaryPartner.com: www.veterinarypartner.com

Humane Organizations

American Society for the Prevention of Cruelty to Animals (ASPCA): 212-876-7700, ext. 4650; www.aspca.org

Humane Society of the United States (HSUS): 202-452-1100; www.hsus.org

Marin Humane Society: 415-883-4621; www.marinhumanesociety.org

San Francisco Society for the Prevention of Cruelty to Animals (SFSPCA): 415-554-3000; www.sfspca.org

Professional Veterinary Organizations

American Animal Hospital Association (AAHA): 303-986-2800; www.aahanet.org *Note: Though primarily for practitioners, the AAHA Web site is a good source of information on the profession for laypersons. Also, go to the association's www.healthypet.com Web site for guidelines and information on aging pets, where you can request a copy of "Senior Moments," a concise brochure on health care for the older pet.*

American Association of Human-Animal Bond Veterinarians (AAH-ABV): http://aahabv.org

American Board of Veterinary Practitioners (ABVP): 800-697-3583; www.abvp.com

American Holistic Veterinary Medical Association (AHVMA): 410-569-0795; www.ahvma.org

American Veterinary Dental College (AVDC): 215-573-8135; www.avdc.org

American Veterinary Medical Association (AVMA): 800-248-2862; www.avma.org *Note: The AVMA site is primarily for members, but public information is available by clicking on the "Care for Animals" and "News" links.*

International Veterinary Academy of Pain Management (IVAPM): 970-297-1257; www.cvmbs.colostate.edu/ivapm *Note: View the online video, "Is Your Pet in Pain?"*

Pet-Related Organizations

American Pet Products Manufacturers Association (APPMA): 203-532-0000; www.appma.org

Association of American Feed Control Officials (AAFCO): www.aafco.org

Pet Food Institute (PFI): 202-367-1120; www.petfoodinstitute.org

Purina Pet Institute: 800-778-7462; www.purina.com/institute

U.S. Food and Drug Administration Center for Veterinary Medicine (CVM): 888-INFO-FDA or 240-276-9300; www.fda.gov/cvm

Pet Supply Companies

GENERAL

Drs. Fosters & Smith: 800-381-7179; www.drsfostersmith.com

PetSmart: 888-839-9638; www.petsmart.com

Senior Pet Products.com: 800-805-2001; www.seniorpetproducts.com

MOBILITY AIDS AND SENIOR-SENSITIVE PRODUCTS

Drs. Foster & Smith: 800-381-7179; www.drsfostersmith.com

Senior Pet Products.com: 800-805-2001; www.seniorpetproducts.com

Pet Insurance and Wellness Programs

Note: These listings are intended only as places to start your research, not as recommendations. The pet insurance industry is still developing, and many of these companies are new on the scene. In all cases, due diligence is required: read the fine print, especially as it applies to older pets and coverage for preexisting conditions.

INSURANCE

PetCare Pet Insurance: 866-275-PETS
www.petcarepals.com

Petshealth Care Plan: 800-807-6724
www.petshealthplan.com

Veterinary Pet Insurance: 800-872-7387
www.petinsurance.com

WELLNESS PROGRAMS

Banfield Optimum Wellness Plan:
866-277-7387
www.petsmart.com/banfield

Pet Assure: 888-789-PETS
www.petassure.com

Pet-Food Cookbooks

Dr. Pitcairn's New Complete Guide to Natural Health for Dogs and Cats, by Richard H. Pitcairn, DVM (Rodale Books, 2005)

Home-Prepared Dog & Cat Diets: The Healthful Alternative, by Donald R. Strombeck (Iowa State University Press, 1999)

Alternative Veterinary Medicine Information

Alternatives for Animals: 810-599-5031; www.alternativesforanimals.com

American Holistic Veterinary Medical Association (AHVMA): 410-569-0795; www.ahvma.org

Feline Cancer Information

Veterinary Cancer Society: 619-474-8929; www.vetcancersociety.org

Perseus Foundation: 651-278-8982; www.perseusfoundation.org

Pain Management Information

International Veterinary Academy of Pain Management at Colorado State University of Veterinary Medicine (IVAPM): 970-297-0344; www.cvmbs.colostate.edu/ivapm

Pfizer Animal Health Division: 800-366-5288; www.pfizerah.com

Pet Hospice Information

Nikki Hospice Foundation for Pets: 707-557-8595; www.pethospice.org

Pet Meds Online

Drs. Foster & Smith: 800-381-7179; www.drsfostersmith.com
Internet Pets: 208-777-2660; www.internetpets.com
National Association of Boards of Pharmacy (NABP): 847-698-6227;
www.nabp.net *Note: Before ordering any of your pet's medicines online, contact the NABP to confirm that the pharmacy is licensed and in good standing.*
Pet Med Express: www.1800PetMed.com

Pet Cemeteries

International Association of Pet Cemeteries and Crematories (IAOPC): 518-594-3000; www.iaopc.com
Moira Allen's Pet Loss Support Web site: www.pet-loss.net
Note: Both these sites also have links to all areas of pet-loss support.

Pet-Loss Support

GENERAL

Association for Pet Loss and Bereavement (APLB): 718-382-0690; www.aplb.org
Farm Animal Welfare Council (FAWC): See the "Five Freedoms" at www.fawc.org.uk/freedoms.htm

SUPPORT HOTLINES

Chicago Veterinary Medical Association: 630-603-3994
Colorado State University Veterinary Teaching Hospital/Argus Institute: 970-297-1242
Cornell University: 607-253-3932
Tufts University, Cummings School of Veterinary Medicine: 508-839-5302
University of California-Davis: 800-565-1526 or 509-335-5704

ONLINE CHAT ROOMS

www.cathobbyist.com/chat
www.pethobbyist.com

BOOKS

Chicken Soup for the Cat & Dog Lover's Soul, by Jack Canfield, Victor Mark Hansen, Marty Becker, DVM, et al. (Health Communications, 1999)
Chicken Soup for the Pet Lover's Soul, and by Jack Canfield, Mark Victor Hansen, Marty Becker, DVM, and Carol Kline (Health Communications, 1998)
The Loss of a Pet, 3rd ed., by Wallace Sife (John Wiley & Sons, Inc., 2005)

BOOKS FOR CHILDREN

I'll Always Love You, by Hans Wilhelm (Crown Books for Young Readers, 1985)
Sad Isn't Bad: A Good-Grief Guidebook for Kids Dealing with Loss, by Michaelene

Mundy; illustrated by Robert W. Alley (Abbey Press, 1998)
When a Pet Dies, by Fred Rogers (Penguin Books for Young Readers, 1998)

Poison Control Information

ASPCA Poison Control Center: 888-426-4435
AVMA "Pet Owner's Guide to Poisons": www.avma.org
Maine Coon Rescue: http://mainecoonrescue.com/poison.html

Senior Citizen–Pet Matchup Programs

Partnering Animals with Seniors (P.A.W.S.): 602-997-7585 or 602-997-7586; www.azhumane.org
Pets for the Elderly Foundation (PEF): 866-849-3598; www.petsfortheelderly.org

Miscellaneous Web Sites

www.aahahelpingpets.org: Or call 866-4HELPETS for information on financial assistance for low-income households.
www.athomevet.org: The Web site of the American Association of Housecall Veterinarians (AAHV), where you can find a vet in your area who makes house calls and performs in-home euthanasia.
http://animalbehaviorcounselors.org: Association of Companion Animal Behavior Counselors (ACABC).
www.barfworld.com: For information on the raw diet, Biologically Appropriate Raw Food (BARF).
www.bravorawdiet.com: For information on the Bravo raw diet.
http://carecredit.com: Or call 800-859-9975 for information on pet health care payment plans.
www.catwellness.org: The Web site of "The Great Cat Watch, for Wellness Sake" campaign to educate cat owners on how to recognize the subtle signs of sickness in their cats.
www.cpr-savers.com: Or call 800-480-1277 for information from CPR Savers & First Aid Supply, which offers wholesale kits of all kinds, including for pets.
www.healthradionetwork.com: Listen to Dr. Marty Becker's weekly radio program, "Top Vets Talk Pets."
www.library.uiuc.edu/vex/vetdocs/abbreviation.htm: Log on here to help decipher those mysterious abbreviations and acronyms.
www.medipet.com: For ready-made first-aid kits; or call 888-633-4738.
www.npwm.com: For information on National Pet Wellness Month.
www.pbs.org/wgbh/nova/vets: Click on "Don't Blame Your Pet," "Ask the Behaviorists," and/or "Resources" for information on pet behavior.
www.petdental.com: For info about National Pet Dental Health Month.
www.Pets911.com: Enter your zip code to find animal shelters, agencies, and other animal care organizations in your community.

Index